BANNER YEAR

How Jayson Tatum, Jaylen Brown, and Brad Stevens Persevered to Lead the Boston Celtics to an Historic 18th Title

Cedric Maxwell
with Mike Isenberg

TRIUMPH
BOOKS

Library of Congress Cataloging-in-Publication Data

Names: Maxwell, Cedric, author. | Isenberg, Mike, author.
Title: Banner year: how Jayson Tatum, Jaylen Brown, and Brad Stevens persevered to lead the Boston Celtics to an historic 18th title / Cedric Maxwell, with Mike Isenberg.
Other titles: How Jayson Tatum, Jaylen Brown, and Brad Stevens persevered to lead the Boston Celtics to an historic eighteenth title
Description: Chicago, Illinois: Triumph Books LLC, [2025]
Identifiers: LCCN 2024058222 | ISBN 9781637278321 (trade paperback)
Subjects: LCSH: Boston Celtics (Basketball team)—History—21st century. | Basketball teams—Massachusetts—Boston—History—21st century. | Basketball—Tournaments—United States—21st century—History. | Tatum, Jayson
Classification: LCC GV885.52.B67 M276 2025 | DDC 796.323/640974461—dc23/eng/20250108
LC record available at https://lccn.loc.gov/2024058222

This book is available in quantity at special discounts for your group or organization. For further information, contact:
Triumph Books LLC
814 North Franklin Street
Chicago, Illinois 60610
(312) 337-0747
www.triumphbooks.com

Printed in U.S.A.
ISBN: 978-1-63727-832-1
Design by Nord Compo
Photos by AP Images

To my kids, Shemeka Maxwell,
Doctor Morgan Maxwell, Madison Maxwell,
and Devin Maxwell

—C.M.

To my wife, Katie; my children, Zach and Cookie;
and best fur friends, Toby and Matilda

—M.I.

CONTENTS

PREFACE

The scoreboard read Miami 103, Boston 84, and believe me—it wasn't that close.

The 2023 Boston Celtics weren't going back to the NBA Finals. A season full of hope? Gone.

Becoming the first team in basketball history to complete a 3–0 comeback? Gone.

As soon as Jayson Tatum rolled his ankle on the Celtics' first possession, the Miami Heat began to roll the weakened Celtics. Somehow Tatum gutted out 41 minutes and 36 seconds and scored 14 points to go with 11 rebounds, but that wasn't nearly enough. The other Jay—Jaylen Brown—couldn't help. Like Tatum, J.B. was All-NBA, but he picked an awful time for his worst game of the season, going 8-of-23 from the floor and turning the ball over *eight* times.

You know the old cliché about how it's always darkest before the dawn?

As I watched the 2024 Celtics demolish the Dallas Mavericks to get over the hump and win the championship,

I had to think back to 385 days earlier, where there sure was a lot of darkness.

It's not like the Jays hadn't had success. Since Tatum joined Brown, who came into the league one year earlier, the dynamic duo had been to the Eastern Conference championship round four times and even led the Golden State Warriors 2–1 in the 2022 NBA Finals. But here in Boston, we measure greatness by one thing: winning the hardware.

The story of the Celtics' 2024 title can best be described in two words: *persistence* and *decisiveness*. They had the persistence to believe in their two young All-Stars and the decisiveness to make the necessary moves to finish the job.

Everyone would have understood if the team decided it had gone as far as it could with the Jays and broken them up. But first Danny Ainge and then Brad Stevens doubled down on Tatum and Brown by adding to the duo. To quote the late Kenny Rogers: "You've got to know when to hold 'em, know when to fold 'em."

Ainge and Stevens played their cards to perfection, and the end result was spectacular.

CHAPTER ONE

THE REBUILD

Prior to the 2007–08 season, Boston Celtics president (and my former teammate) Danny Ainge rolled the dice and came up with a lucky seven—or, in his case, 17. By putting all his chips to the center of the table, Ainge got Kevin Garnett and Ray Allen to go with Paul Pierce—all future Hall of Famers—along with Rajon Rondo and Kendrick Perkins to blow away the rest of the NBA and win their 17th title, the most in league history.

This group would get to another Finals, but injury and age took their toll, and by 2013 things were a mess. Allen and Rondo didn't get along. So Allen had left the previous year, joining our archrival, the Miami Heat. A first-round playoff loss to the New York Knicks emphasized that the days of dominance had come to an end. The future wasn't bright, and head coach Doc Rivers was looking for a way out despite having just signed a contract extension. "Doc didn't really want to rebuild, and it's hard to blame him," current Celtics assistant general manager Austin Ainge recalled. "I mean, losing is no fun, man. It's hard. And you need to be fully invested in it and have a long-term energy. And if you're not into it, then it's probably better to not be part of it because...rebuilding is hard. It's hard on players, coaches, front office, ownership, and fanbases. It's hard on everybody. Sometimes it's the best move, but it's a hard process."

Danny Ainge never did anything half-assed. So with Allen and now Doc gone, it was time to finish clearing the decks.

* * *

If you look through the history of the Boston Celtics, championship runs usually start with a big trade. In 1956 Red Auerbach traded Cliff Hagan and Ed Macauley to the St. Louis Hawks for a draft pick who would become the great Bill Russell. Early in my career, Auerbach swindled the Golden State Warriors into giving us Kevin McHale and Robert Parish in exchange for a couple of first-round picks.

Then in the aforementioned 2007 heist, Danny Ainge traded nearly half the roster—five players and multiple picks—to the Minnesota Timberwolves to acquire Kevin Garnett and then sent three more players to the Seattle SuperSonics for Ray Allen. The second Big Three was born.

Over the years Ainge has often been quoted that he thought Auerbach had made a mistake by holding on to Larry Bird, McHale, and Parish too long, that he should have traded them for more assets while they still had value.

Bob Ryan, the legendary writer for *The Boston Globe*, won the Curt Gowdy Media Award from the Naismith Memorial Basketball Hall of Fame. "It was still pretty cold-blooded," Ryan said, flashing back to the early 1990s. "You're talking about that the one of the three who would have been the least-mourned sentimentally was Robert. Obviously, Larry, you can't even remotely entertain the idea of getting rid of Larry Bird. Kevin, not quite the same level but still a high level. Robert would have been the one they would have been willing to sacrifice, if you will, just because he was the third in the order of that Big Three."

Ainge wasn't going to let history repeat itself. With the Big Three era coming to an end, he was at it again, completing a franchise-changing deal with the Brooklyn Nets, and that formed the foundation of the 2024 championship team led by Jaylen Brown and Jayson Tatum. When all was said and done, the Nets got K.G., Paul Pierce, Jason Terry, D.J. White, and a 2017 draft pick swap. Brooklyn was where KG and Pierce wanted to go; both sides worked together, including agents, along with Nets star Deron Williams.

We ended up with five mostly forgettable players but three first-round picks and a draft pick swap. "I remember being in the war room, which was our Celtics board room in the Boston office," team owner Wyc Grousbeck told *The Globe* shortly after the deal. "Danny came in and said, 'I've got a trade worked out for Pierce and Garnett to go to Brooklyn.' I think we originally were going to get one unprotected first-round pick, I said, 'Go back and get another one.' I don't normally do that in trades, but my reading of the situation was that the owner of the Nets was a newer owner [Mikhail Prokhorov], and he was very gung ho—as I am—in that it's all about winning."

Ryan points out that though this trade was huge, it wasn't quite the Russell or McHale/Parish deals. "I'm not sure everybody was crying about it," he said. "They recognized it was a move that not only had to be made, but it was an alternative to what was going on. Maybe I'm wrong, but I don't think about it that much anywhere near on the level of those other two deals."

History will show Boston ending up with Brown and Tatum, but at the time, the verdict wasn't so clear. "We thought the Nets were going to be very good and we thought we were getting some late picks the first few years and then have a chance to maybe sneak one in the tail end," Austin Ainge said. "That was kind of our best-case scenario mindset. And it just didn't work out as well for them, and we got lucky."

Nobody could have imagined they'd get *that* lucky.

With K.G. and Pierce chasing a title in Brooklyn, the next job in Boston was to find a new on-court leader. That's when Danny Ainge made a move that nobody expected—hiring Butler's 36-year-old Brad Stevens as head coach. I'm not going to lie. I knew absolutely nothing about this Stevens guy and, to be honest, I don't think most of the people in the organization did either.

It just so happened that Stevens was one of the best coaches in college—he'd led Butler to consecutive NCAA championship games—but he was so understated. He had a pretty low profile. "Obviously, he's very smart, he understands the game very well, but also he has tremendous personal character, leadership, and humility despite all of his success. He had the humility required. And that sounds maybe not like the most important characteristic for a coach, but to us it was," Austin Ainge said. "College coaches sometimes become like small-town mayors. They kind of really run everything. They run, they pick the team. They're very, very powerful in their little sphere of influence in college. And in the NBA, it's more of a collaborative approach…You have to work with your star players who are powerful. You have to work with medical staff, analytics staff, front offices, ownership. You have to be more collaborative and cooperative. For a college coach to be successful, we thought he had to have a degree of humility and ability to work with others to really make it. And besides Brad's great coaching resume, that was a thing that stuck out to us."

Ryan was shocked by the news of Stevens' hiring. "Stunning, stunning, stunning, stunning because he just seemed so perfectly collegian and so perfectly in his element. He was so perfect for their sensibility and their self-image and Butler," he said. "There was no idea that there was any professional interest at all. Turns out he had, and we didn't know. He was quiet about it, and Danny really conducted the negotiations brilliantly. But he had apparently. Some people did know he may have had professional aspirations, but most of us, I think, had no idea that he would be interested in the NBA, that he was definitely going to be a college guy for life."

And for Stevens, who was in a very comfortable situation at Butler, this wasn't an easy decision. "It took me nine days to decide to do it. It seems like a no-brainer to people when you talk about the Celtics, right?" Stevens said. "How much of an honor and how flattering it is to get called by a team with this tradition and in this city where it matters this much."

He, though, wasn't intimidated by the idea of a rebuild. In fact, naivete was helpful in this case. "I probably was a little oblivious to how far we were when I first took the job just because I was new to the NBA. I knew trading Garnett,

Pierce, and Jason Terry probably wouldn't be good for winning," he said, stating the obvious. Plus, he had a fallback. "I was 36 and I didn't look at it as, *Most college coaches don't make it or get let go or anything else.* I looked at it as, *Well, if I don't, then I'll just go back to college.* I didn't see it to be a huge downside."

Stevens was certainly looking for the best talent, but if you spend five minutes talking with him, you know he values character nearly as much. "I did think that if we get the right people in the building and we emphasize the right things and we work really hard, then we'll maximize ourselves to the best of our ability," he said. "It didn't take long to do that, and we've always prioritized those good people."

So that covers the type of players the new coach was looking for, but that was just a piece of the pie—a big piece—but when you take a job like that, you need to make sure management is going to have your back. "The most important question that I wanted to know was: who am I working with and how committed are they to the process that it takes to be good? How patient are we with going through the ups and downs of that process? And there are some painful times, and the pain only increases when you're really good…It's not that bad when you're just kind of trying to figure out if you're any good, right?" Stevens said. "I do think that it's important not to ride the roller coaster. It's important to evaluate things evenly. It's important to see it, listen to every perspective but also do it without emotion."

To go out and get Stevens, it just shows the level of sophistication and preparation with which Ainge did his job.

He was so ahead of the game when it came to hiring guys; it was incredible.

Stevens' first team was a collection of random names I can barely remember. Sure, Rajon Rondo was there, but so were guys like Kris Humphries, Jordan Crawford, and Joel Anthony. It was no surprise they went 24–57. But it only took seven games into a lost season for me to think, *Maybe this Stevens guy is the right coach for this organization.*

We were in Miami against the two-time defending champions, and somehow the game was close. Time was running down, and Stevens drew up a play with a couple of seconds left on the clock, and we had the ball at halfcourt. Gerald Wallace threw a beautifully timed pass to Jeff Green, who caught it and knocked down the winning three-pointer at the buzzer.

Everyone was watching this incredible play, but I was also watching Stevens. The ball went through the hoop, everyone was jumping around, but Stevens waved to Miami Heat coach Erik Spoelstra and walked off the court. There wasn't any excitement from Stevens. Now maybe there was some in the locker room, but he was totally cool while leaving the court. He was exactly who I wanted at the helm. Stevens has that demeanor, just very calm, very understated, which wasn't common back then. I think coaches have changed, and it's off of Stevens' blueprint. Look at Joe Mazzulla today and you see the same thing.

Stevens inherited a roster that was down to the studs, and Rondo was ready to lose his mind. Those Celtics tied for the fourth worst record in the league. Remember what I said about it being darkest before dawn? Well, this was the calm before the storm.

The next couple of seasons saw incremental improvements, winning 40 and 48 games, and Danny Ainge's bold moves were about to pay off.

CHAPTER TWO

BUILT TO WIN

BUILT TO WIN

In 2016 the Boston Celtics went 48–34. Somehow, Brad Stevens coached a team of misfits with the likes of Isaiah Thomas, Jonas Jerebko, Jae Crowder, and Marcus Smart—to the fifth seed for the Eastern Conference playoffs. The "super team" in Brooklyn, meanwhile—with Kevin Garnett and Paul Pierce long gone—struggled to a 21–61 record. That gave Boston the third pick in the NBA draft, and Danny Ainge took a relatively unknown freshman forward from Cal, a guy by the name of Jaylen Brown.

The following season the Celtics had the best record in the East, while the Brooklyn Nets ended up with the worst record in the entire league. After the lottery Ainge had the first pick in the draft. Eventually, that turned into another guy, Jayson Tatum. Let's just say things worked out pretty well.

Brown was the savior in the 2024 Eastern Conference Finals. His ridiculous three-pointer in Game One not only saved the Celtics' bacon, but also really set the tone for their sweep.

For J.B. to be "that guy" is easy to see now, but it's crazy to think back to when he came into the league because he was a guy who couldn't hit the side of a barn in Summer League before his rookie season. Now he's turned into this unbelievable shooter. I mean, he hit one of the greatest shots in Celtics history.

It might seem like drafting Brown was a no-brainer, but you have to go back to that night.

The Philadelphia 76ers had the top pick and took the consensus No. 1 prospect, Ben Simmons. (How'd that work out? LOL.) Duke's Brandon Ingram (from my hometown of Kinston, North Carolina,) then went to the Los Angeles Lakers. Three years later, he was sent to the New Orleans Pelicans as part of a package for Anthony Davis.

Among the names available for the Celtics were Jamal Murray and future All-Stars Domantas Sabonis and Pascal Siakam. "It wasn't that simple. Jaylen didn't have a great second half of his freshman year at Cal, but I remained a fan of his through the ups and downs," Ainge told *The Boston Globe*. "We knew what he was well before he got to college."

Austin Ainge had seen Brown play on an All-Star team in Italy before college. He felt that J.B.'s inconsistency at Cal was more a case of a mismatched roster. "He had a non-shooting point guard and then two non-shooting bigs in the paint," Austin Ainge said. "I mean, they had a lot of talent. They were a very good team, a collection of individual talents, but the talents didn't fit very well together."

But the faith of Austin's father, Danny, in Brown helped land the plane. "Leading up to that draft, he kept telling the rest of our staff because we had wavered because of Jaylen had some bad games, especially toward the end of the year," Austin said. "The conference tournament didn't go well. And he said, 'Guys, just keep watching.' And we all got there eventually and we were all on board with the Jaylen pick. But I don't think we would have gotten there necessarily without his confidence in Jaylen."

One thing that impressed the Celtics' brass was that Brown wasn't afraid to work out against anyone. Even today a lot of guys only do drills, not wanting to risk looking bad. That confidence was a big part of what pushed him over the future Denver Nuggets star, Murray.

"Murray was a real strong consideration," Austin said. "But after Jaylen's draft workouts in Boston, it was unanimous that Jaylen was our guy."

The next year, by virtue of the Nets' swap—and winning the draft lottery—Boston had the top overall pick. Everyone agreed that Markelle Fultz was the big prize. The shooting guard from the University of Washington was the consensus top pick. Again, revisionist history shows that Fultz ended up being an average player at best. But Austin said Fultz received strong consideration for us. "We loved Markelle Fultz also very much through the process," Austin said. "[He] was a very talented prospect, and we were very high on him. I would say when we got the No. 1 pick in the lottery when the lottery happened, I bet you most of us probably thought we would take Markelle at that point."

But over the coming days after meeting Tatum, working him out, checking his background, the Celtics had their mind made up on the soft-spoken Duke star. Like most blue-chip prospects, Tatum only spent one year in Durham, North Carolina, and as Austin recalls, he got better as that season went on. "Jayson had kind of a rough start. He got injured early on, and then his second half of the year was much better. And you could really see his growth and his maturity," Austin said. "Jayson is very smart and calm and a good person, just all the things that you want to build and have in your program."

Knowing that Philadelphia (aka "The Process") wanted Fultz, Danny Ainge worked out a deal to drop down to the third spot and add a first rounder the next season. The Sixers selected Fultz—then traded him two seasons later. Meanwhile, the Celtics got a future Hall of Famer.

In the span of two drafts—thanks in large part to the Nets—Danny Ainge had reloaded for the next great Celtics team. As much as he gets credit for executing the trade and coming out with the picks that turned out to be his franchise cornerstones, he also needs to take a bow for not giving in to his impulses.

As he told Quentin Richardson on his podcast, Danny was hellbent on getting a star, and the guy he targeted was Jimmy Butler, who was with the Chicago Bulls at the time. Danny said he regretted not drafting Butler back in 2011 and he had a chance to finally get his man. Such a trade would've cost him the chance to select Brown and Tatum. "I was trying to get Jimmy Butler from Chicago when I was in Boston, but they wanted a lot. And so we didn't do it. It…would've been Jaylen and Jayson, both those draft picks," Danny recalled. "I loved Jimmy and was trying to get him, could have drafted Jimmy late. I liked him even then. He'd been proving that, how good of a player he was. That was probably one [regret]."

It's safe to say that had Ainge made the deal, *that* would have been his biggest regret.

* * *

By Brad Stevens' fourth year, we finally signed a big free agent, Al Horford, and had actually gotten the top seed in the East before falling in the Eastern Conference Finals in five mostly non-competitive games to LeBron James and the Cleveland Cavaliers.

Prior to Big Al coming on board, the Celtics had never been big players in free agency. Probably the biggest name we signed was back in 1994 with 35-year-old Dominique Wilkins.

Although the media portrays Boston as a place that free agents don't necessarily want to go to, Austin Ainge says it's really more situation-driven. "The Celtics just for years had not chosen to go clear cap space. I'm talking long before my dad took over. There were all these stats [that it has] been this long since Celtics signed a free agent, and we felt that that was just more their decisions about the cap and trade more than anything about Boston or the Celtics or the city," he said. "We feel like even years before we got Al, that players wanted to be in Boston and be traded to us, and agents would work with us to help us. And that it was just kind of a happenstance of management's philosophy that prevented any big free-agent signings. But we felt like Kevin Garnett was essentially a free agent signing…He had to choose to come and extend. It's just kind of like a salary cap asterisk that Al Horford was the first one in a while."

After signing Horford, Danny Ainge made his next big moves, first signing All-Star Gordon Hayward—who starred under Brad Stevens at Butler—to a massive four-year contract worth nearly $128 million.

But that was just the appetizer. Then he traded All-NBA guard Isaiah Thomas, who had just finished fifth in MVP voting while averaging 28.9 points per game, to the Cavaliers for Kyrie Irving. Suddenly, we were the team to beat—at least in the East, if not in the entire league. We had three legitimate stars in Horford, Hayward, and Irving with a rookie named Jayson Tatum, a second-year player in Jaylen Brown, and solid players like Marcus Smart and Terry Rozier.

The sky was the limit.

Until the sky came crashing down five minutes into the opening game.

Hayward suffered a nasty ankle injury that would end his season and change the course of his career. That night Charles Barkley said there was no way the Celtics would even make the playoffs. Stevens really earned his stripes that season, as we somehow ended up winning 55 games, getting the second seed. As if they didn't have enough to overcome, Irving needed knee surgery in March and was done for the year. But this group *still* wouldn't give up. We actually led the Cavs in Game Seven of the Eastern Conference Finals with six minutes to go, and this game also had an iconic dunk by the 20-year-old Tatum over James. (Check it out on YouTube.)

In the end experience won out—along with James' 35 points, 15 rebounds, and nine assists—and the Cavs advanced to the Finals, where they were swept by the Golden State Warriors.

* * *

With Kyrie Irving and Gordon Hayward healthy, we were *the* team to beat the next season. But as great a coach as Brad Stevens already was, he was *not* a finished product. There's a huge difference between coaching at a small school like Butler versus being the coach of the Boston Celtics—especially with a target on your back after those marquee acquisitions.

The Jays were a year older and more experienced. We oozed talent. Too much talent, as it turned out. You can only play five guys at a time—something USA Basketball coach Steve Kerr would learn with Jayson Tatum years later. I think Stevens was trying to run a democracy, to play everybody. The guys on the second unit were averaging 15 to 20 minutes a game, and you've still got to get the starters going. The math simply didn't work. If there was one fault I think Stevens had, it's that he was too sensitive to every player's needs and desires. That's impossible to do, which I learned early in my career.

When Bill Fitch took over our team in 1979, he made it clear who the boss was. He didn't give a fuck about players eight, nine, or 10. His attitude was: "You guys fit in when you get in." Fitch knew games were going to be won with Larry Bird, Robert Parish, (eventually) Kevin McHale, Tiny Archibald, and myself. Everyone else filled specific roles. This also happened when Doc Rivers was leading the Celtics to the title. At one point, Kendrick Perkins and Rajon Rondo complained about their roles in the offense. Doc made it clear he didn't care what they were thinking. It was about Kevin Garnett, Paul Pierce, and Ray Allen. He was going to ride them and then fill in the rest.

It took 2018 for Stevens to learn that lesson. He had Irving, one of the best players in the league. Hayward was back, and it's easy to forget, but he was one hell of a player. Not a good one, a great one. Tatum and Jaylen Brown were coming on strong; they'd just led an injury-depleted team to within six minutes of the NBA Finals. Think about those players and tell me how you slice up playing time. Hell, Morris—a serviceable vet—averaged 28 minutes a game. That was more than Brown! Let that one sink in.

It put an incredible amount of stress on Stevens. He basically had too much talent.

"We had Terry Rozier and Marcus Morris and a lot of dudes on our bench. We struggled to get them all minutes and touches," Austin Ainge said. "It got a little challenging… Jayson and Jaylen were kind of the focal points and the stars. We wanted some veteran complementary pieces that fit them."

Years later, when Stevens was in the front office and Joe Mazzulla took over on the bench, Austin pointed out that it was a different situation. The Jays were clearly established, and roles were defined. That's the thing I love about Mazzulla. He made the decision that someone like Payton Pritchard gets not many minutes. Maybe he takes two half-court shots to end quarters. Maybe he gets another three-to-four shots, but that's it. When somebody gets hurt, he might play more.

Stevens learned from the 2018–19 season. I mean Morris had a great year, but he played *a lot* of minutes. Stevens figured out how to differentiate and take people out of the game.

CHAPTER THREE

THE KYRIE EXPERIENCE

The move to acquire Kyrie Irving was a bold move by the organization. Isaiah Thomas represented one of Danny Ainge's truly incredible finds. The last pick in the 2011 NBA Draft, I.T. had put together a decent—if unspectacular—career with the Sacramento Kings and Phoenix Suns during his first four seasons. When Ainge worked out a three-way trade, essentially giving up a first-round pick and some roster fillers to get him, nobody paid that close of attention except to wonder why Ainge would do something like that.

The answer came pretty quickly. In two-plus seasons, Thomas averaged 24 points a game, became a two-time All-Star, and finished fifth in the MVP voting. But I guess the team figured it had gone as far as it could with a go-to player who was only 5'9", and Irving was looking to leave LeBron James and the Cleveland Cavaliers.

Everyone knew Irving; he was the first overall pick in that same 2011 NBA Draft, he won Rookie of the Year, was a four-time All-Star, and, of course, hit one of the biggest shots in NBA Finals history to give the Cavs their first and only title. Sure, he was a little bit quirky. (He argued the world was flat.) And he never made it clear why he'd leave such a good team, but according to reports, he wanted out, and the desired locations were San Antonio, Minnesota, Miami, or

New York. Ainge ignored the noise and made the deal. To get a talent like that in exchange for Thomas (who needed hip surgery), Jae Crowder, a European prospect, and a couple of picks? That seemed to be a no-brainer.

Things started out great for Irving in Boston. In that first season, he averaged more than 24 points and five assists a game. But it was clear that the organization was bending over backward to make Irving happy so that he'd re-sign when his contract was up after two years.

In fact, before he second season in Boston, he spoke at an event held at the TD Garden. Irving talked about having his number hanging from the rafters one day. His famous quote was: "If you guys will have me back, I plan on re-signing here." (Note: that didn't age well.)

I think everyone allowed Irving to do some things that maybe shouldn't have been done. It was like there were rules for the team and separate ones for Irving. Every year the Boston Celtics have a tip-off banquet before the season opener. It's a chance for fans to meet the players, get pictures, get autographs, etc. They've been doing it forever. I'll be damned if there wasn't security around Irving so nobody could approach him. So much for fan access.

As you can imagine, the team does a ton of stuff for charity. One time they were passing around basketballs to get all the players to sign them. And they all did—except for Irving. It felt like every day the team just pampered and tried to appease him, and I think it was draining for everyone. Now don't get me wrong—Irving is an unbelievable player, but his track record speaks for itself. I remember when he signed with the Brooklyn Nets and his buddy, Kevin Durant. Irving told everyone that they really didn't need a coach. I'm sure the guy who *did* coach the Nets—Hall of Famer Steve Nash—really appreciated that.

The crazy part is that when you talk to some people in the front office, they say he was the nicest guy in the world to deal with. "Our guys still have decent relationships with Kyrie," Austin Ainge said. "It went really well for a year and a half and then it kind of frayed there toward the end. To be honest, I still don't fully understand or know why. I've heard different versions from all involved, but you know he was a very good player and very talented and, for whatever reason, he wasn't super happy with us and wanted to leave."

That sums up the Kyrie Irving experience. As hard as it was to deal with Irving, coaching him didn't seem like a whole lot of fun either. I think Brad Stevens' nature didn't help him in this instance. Stevens has never been a confrontational or controversial guy. He never liked players getting on each other's asses, he wouldn't show anyone up. Things were different in my day. Not only did Bill Fitch have no problem lighting us up, but we also policed each other. If something wasn't right, I'd say, "Damn it, Chief, you do this!" or "Larry, we're going to do this!" Looking back, between Stevens' nature and where the Jays were in their evolution, it's easy to see how Irving ran amok.

Once Irving left Boston in 2019 (after his pledge to return), Danny Ainge did a sign-and-trade with the Charlotte Hornets, sending Terry Rozier out in exchange for Kemba Walker, who was a great player in his own right but dealt with major knee issues in Boston. Still, he was a good tonic for the team after the Kyrie Irving experience.

* * *

The 2019–20 season was, of course, disrupted by Covid-19. Everything was shut down for a few months, and the playoffs took place in a bubble near Walt Disney World.

The Jays both played really well in the Eastern Conference Finals against the Miami Heat, but Gordon Hayward got hurt again, Kemba Walker was a shell of himself because of the knee, and the Heat won in six games. Jimmy Butler, whom Danny Ainge had tried to trade for, showed he was worth his new contract, and role players like Duncan Robinson made themselves a whole lot of money. The Boston Celtics had been in three of the last four Eastern Conference Finals but hadn't been able to break through.

Jayson Tatum was named third team All-NBA, and Jaylen Brown was coming on strong, finishing his first season of averaging 20 points a game. As the country was beginning to inch back to normal, we looked pretty damn strong.

Things never really clicked, though. Walker was limited to 43 games (out of 72), Marcus Smart only played 48, and Brown suffered a wrist injury, which kept him out of 14—and the playoffs. It was no surprise when Kevin Durant, Kyrie Irving, and the Brooklyn Nets blew us away in five easy games.

Of course, Irving couldn't just take the win.

The Nets took the first two games and then came to Boston. Before Game Three Irving told ESPN, "Hopefully, we can just keep it strictly basketball; there's no belligerence or racism going on—subtle racism," Irving said. "People yelling shit from the crowd, but even if it is, it's part of the nature of the game, and we're just going to focus on what we can control."

After Brooklyn smoked us in Game Four 141–126, Irving decided to stomp on the Celtics logo at midcourt.

We figured something was going to change but had no idea of what was to come.

CHAPTER FOUR

PRESIDENT STEVENS AND COACH UDOKA

The date was June 2, 2021. A bombshell was about to drop in Boston. Danny Ainge shocked the world and announced his retirement as president of the Boston Celtics. Even as a former teammate and current friend, I was stunned.

Ainge cited health and family as reasons he stepped down. He'd had a heart attack two years earlier, which led him to start thinking about what he was doing with his life. "You're surrounded by your six children in the hospital, and they say, 'Hey you need to stop doing this.' I don't know what my future holds. I don't have any plans," he said.

One of those six sons added more insight. "The simple answer is he was just done operating the day to day," Austin Ainge said. "It's a very, very big job, and he was ready to step back from making all these decisions every day...I mean he loves the draft, trades, free agency, and that stuff. But you're managing a big staff, you're the day-to-day CEO of a whole organization. You're dealing with chefs, trainers, doctors, equipment managers, and travel with every headache...He was just done with that in Boston. It was going to be hard to change that when everyone's used to going to him for 20 years in Boston."

Danny later told *The Boston Globe*'s Dan Shaughnessy: "I just felt like I needed a break, well before the playoffs started, and I also felt like the team was in great hands. When I decided to walk, I didn't think that Brad [Stevens] would take over my spot. I thought that Brad would still be coaching."

I wasn't surprised at all when seven months later, Danny returned home to Utah to work with good friend (and Jazz owner) Ryan Smith, where he's the CEO of basketball operations.

But was there another shoe to drop? Taking Danny's place was…Brad Stevens. One of the best coaches in the NBA was now going upstairs to run the organization.

Stevens said that when Danny first told management of his plan to step aside, he had a meeting with Danny and ownership to figure out who the team wanted to target as a replacement.

There were internal and external options, and the team spoke with most, if not all, of them. In fact, Stevens thinks the team may have offered the job to one or two of them.

Because of their close relationship, Stevens had an intimate look at what Danny was doing over the years, which piqued his curiosity. "I just said kind of in passing that, 'Hey, at some point in time, I'm gonna be needing a break from coaching,'" Stevens said. "And this is something that I've always enjoyed and been interested in, and that is the team building aspect.'"

Stevens' self-awareness and humility—two traits that helped him get the coaching job—were evident in discussions about becoming team president. He told everyone that he'd need a lot of technical help—things like managing the salary cap, procedures, and protocols. But when you think about it, it made all the sense in the world. "I did need a break from coaching," Stevens said. "And at the same time, I knew the team. I knew the guys in the room. I had an idea of what I thought would make them be the best fits around them, but executing that and actually getting some of these guys is really difficult."

And with two young children, it helped. Because by calling the shots, it allowed him to make his own schedule. He said that he hardly ever missed one of his kids' games. As tempting as the promotion was, Stevens always put the team first. "Hiring a new coach will give us a great opportunity to hire somebody that will be…a new, fresh voice with a new, fresh perspective," Stevens said. "They don't have to fill Doc Rivers' shoes like I did. And they don't have to fill Danny Ainge's shoes like I do. They just have to figure out a way to be better than the last guy."

Austin Ainge goes back to why the team hired Stevens in the first place as to why ownership made this choice. "It's the same thing that made his transition from college to the NBA world, the same skillset. He knew the game, knew the league. He knows what wins," Austin said. "So, all of that was easy for him…He just came in with humility and asked a lot of questions and wasn't scared to ask for help in certain situations and learned it all extremely fast, and I think became one of the best GMs in the league in a very short time."

Promoting Stevens to team president made sense; everyone knew how smart he was and how hard he worked. I go back to former New England Patriots coach Bill Parcells' famous line: "If they want you to cook the dinner, at least they ought to let you shop for some of the groceries."

I was extremely surprised to see Stevens leave coaching to go into that position, but he knew what was in the damn refrigerator. If anyone had to go buy those groceries, Stevens was the perfect guy because he'd been there. He knew the team, the weaknesses, and nuances. He had all those things down.

The first thing President Stevens did was to fix an unfortunate situation. In July of 2019, Al Horford left the Celtics for a four-year, $97 million deal with the Philadelphia 76ers, who thought he'd be a great fit next to their franchise player, Joel Embiid. They were wrong. Big Al and Embiid were a clunky fit, and the team sent him to Oklahoma City after just one year in Philly.

The Oklahoma City Thunder had salary cap room, figured he'd be a good veteran presence, and got a first-round pick out of the deal. Horford was revitalized in OKC and played pretty well until he was shut down by the team. Team executives knew the Thunder were in a major rebuild, and the more Horford played, the greater chance he had of injury, diminishing an asset. Either way they weren't making the playoffs, so why not tank all the way, right?

Stevens saw an opening and didn't want to wait—even though he still had no head coach.

Boston wanted to get out of paying the last season of Kemba Walker's deal since he was so badly diminished. So the Thunder sent Horford to the Celtics for Walker—basically an exchange of bad contracts—plus a first-round pick. Sure, Horford wasn't getting any younger, but Stevens figured that after sitting out nearly half the season his body would be fresh. Plus, he knew what kind of teammate Horford was. OKC also got what it wanted: yet another pick to rebuild with.

* * *

When news broke of Brad Stevens moving upstairs, there were reports the team was considering folks like Jason Kidd and Chauncey Billups as head coach, but the name that quickly surfaced was Ime Udoka. He had spent parts of seven seasons as an NBA journeyman. He then became an assistant coach, working with the San Antonio Spurs, Philadelphia 76ers, and Brooklyn Nets. As he told Yahoo Sports, this wasn't his first go-around, and he was excited about the opportunity with a contending team. "Detroit, Indiana, Cleveland," Udoka said, "I can go down the list. That was tough because I believe I was ready. There are only 30 teams, and I get that, but to not be in a rebuild and being in an expectation pressure-filled situation, I wouldn't trade that in any day."

He was clearly happy to be a part of the winningest franchise in the NBA. "The one thing I would say is the disappointment of coming in second a few years really hurt," Udoka said. "But if you told me I'd have to wait for Boston and get [bypassed] by some of the ones that I got beat out on, it's a no-brainer for me. I'm happy to be in Boston."

Not one to sugarcoat things, he bluntly outlined his plan of attack during his introductory news conference. "We want to have a well-rounded team," Udoka said. "[I] looked at the numbers overall. Sorry to mention this, Brad, but 27th in assists last year—we want to have more team basketball there. But at the same time, you have to understand what your personnel dictates, and that's Jayson, Jaylen, and guys that can really score the basketball at an elite level. You play toward their strengths."

He was a hard ass, and I think the hope was that after Stevens' gentle touch that Udoka's no-bullshit approach would bring the Jays to the next level. "Obviously, we'll have a defensive mentality going in," said Udoka when he met the media. "I like to try to bring the dog out in guys, and we got some young dogs here and look forward to pushing them."

The team got off to a slow start, going 2–5 in its first seven games. It seemed like things were crashing on the night of that seventh game, when we blew a 19-point second-half lead to the Chicago Bulls, losing by 14. Marcus Smart, one of the few vocal leaders in the group, had seen enough. "Every team knows we are trying to go to Jayson and Jaylen, and every team is programmed and studied to stop Jayson and Jaylen," he said. "Everybody's scouting report is to make those guys try to pass the ball." Then Smart dropped the money line: "They don't want to pass the ball, and that's something that they're going to learn. They're still learning, and we're proud of the progress they are making, but they are going to have to make another step and find ways to not only create for themselves, but create for others on this team to open up the court for them later in the game where they don't always have to take those tough shots or take tough matchups when they do get the one-on-one and see a trap."

In that Bulls game, the Jays combined for 40 shots; the rest of the team took 46. "It's something that we've been asking for them to do, and they're learning. We just got to continue to help those guys do that and to help our team. There's only so much I can do without the ball in my hands. I'm just standing in the corner," Smart said. "We're running plays for our best players; every team knows that. They do a good job of shutting that down. We can't allow that. When they shut that down, we can't keep trying to go to those guys."

I know it's the new millennium, and you don't see guys calling out their teammates, but I think that they should have that in their arsenal. They can point and look at guys and say, "We or you did not do that." The Jays were the darlings of the team, and Smart was looked at as the bad cop anyway. When something happened on the floor, he was usually in the middle of it. That was his M.O. "That's the thing about Smart: he wasn't going to change," said respected sportswriter Bob Ryan. "It is a different generation, and there's not much of that anymore from anybody. It's just that's not the way they are. Smart was a throwback, that's for sure."

I was thrilled when Smart called out Brown and Tatum, and my guess is that Udoka relished it, too. Stevens really frowned on guys calling each other out. It was team, team, team. But sometimes in a game or a season, you've got to get on somebody's ass. During the 1984 Finals, Larry Bird called all of us out, saying that we needed heart transplants, and we were a bunch of sissies. And you know what? He was right! We had just lost by 33 points and looked pathetic. We came out and won the next game on the road against the Los Angeles Lakers.

One thing you see with great teams is that they hold everyone accountable. When Dennis Johnson first came to Boston, our coach, K.C. Jones, called him out one day during practice.

D.J. came to a few of the guys, bitching about how Case had treated him. I'm sure D.J. was expecting for his teammates to have his back, but he was in the wrong—not Jones. We told him that, and it sent the message that this was how we operate: we do things the right way. K.C. and D.J. never had another problem again.

And just like his point guard, Udoka wasn't taking any shit, and he had the backing of Stevens. That reminds me of another NBA anecdote. When LeBron James and the Miami Heat got off to a rough start in year one, he went to Pat Riley and asked him to take over as coach, replacing the young, unproven Erik Spoelstra. Riley had done that years earlier with Stan Van Gundy and won his last title on the bench. This time, though, Riley told James that Spo wasn't going anywhere.

There weren't going to be any rumors going on like that with us, which Stevens made clear. "The one thing that I should be good at is supporting the head coach and not being involved," Stevens said just before he hired Udoka. "My door is open, but I do not want to be anything but supportive. In a weird way, in kind of a messed-up way, I'm looking forward to the first time we lose, and I can walk in there and put my arm around him and say, 'I've lost a ton here. Let's go get a coffee. Let's go grab a beer. It's okay. It's part of a long journey.' I'm looking forward to that just being a support and staying out of it from a coaching perspective."

Udoka wasn't afraid to call guys out, and if they didn't like it? Tough luck. He established himself as *the* coach. I felt like he would be here for the next eight to 10 years. There was no question in my mind. That mentality was a throwback to my time in the league. Coaches today don't challenge players anymore. Udoka had no qualms about doing that.

I remember back when Doc Rivers was coaching here, and the team was terrible. Doc's fuse was about to blow. Paul

Pierce hadn't gotten back on defense after missing a shot, and Doc had seen enough. This was in the second half of the game, but Doc pulled his star and sat his ass on the bench. Pierce sat there for a bit with steam coming out of his ears. He was pissed.

Finally, Doc went up to P.P. and said, "Damn it, you ready to play now?" Pierce shrugged his shoulders and went back into the game. The point had been made.

Udoka was certainly cut from the same cloth. He gave off this attitude of "Don't fuck with Grandpa!" He earned the team's respect instantly, and they responded. Udoka was like that teacher who came to your room on the first day of class when you're messing around, doing whatever you want. He came in, and all of the sudden, they're going to stop what they're doing for however long he's here.

I had a teacher like that named Mr. Little. Let's just say he didn't play. And this was back in the day when corporal punishment was allowed. We'd screw around, but when Mr. Little came in, it was the quietest room in the school. We knew that if we acted up, Mr. Little would give us two choices: he'd either beat us with a ruler or make us stand there with our arms raised and two huge encyclopedias in our hands for 15 minutes. Udoka was like the modern-day Mr. Little.

* * *

After losing on January 21 to the Portland Trail Blazers, we stood at 23–24. Things didn't look great. But then something happened. At the trade deadline, Brad Stevens

continued his aggressiveness, dealing former first-round pick
Romeo Langford (who incidentally was chosen with the pick
Stevens pilfered from the Philadelphia 76ers) and a future
first-rounder for guard Derrick White.

When people ask me what I knew about White at the
time, I'll be honest—I only knew that the brother had a
bad Afro that needed to be cut. We'd played him a couple
of times in San Antonio, but there was nothing remarkable
about his game. He was basically just another guy. Even a
hoops junkie like Bob Ryan was stumped. I absolutely didn't
know anything about where he came from. I didn't know
about the small college background. I didn't know that he
had just averaged 14 points a game.

Ryan said that White had been understated his whole
NBA career. "He just slinked his way in the league rather
unnoticed," he said. "And fortunately for him, he went to
play for Pop."

It was also fortunate for the Boston Celtics, as White's
assistant coach for his first couple of years on those San
Antonio Spurs teams? A guy named Ime Udoka.

In White's first game in green, he hit three three-pointers
for a home win vs. the Denver Nuggets, but he struggled
overall. As he settled in, the team took off. The guys bought
into Udoka's defensive philosophy, and the Jays started playing
more of an all-around game. When the playoffs started, the
Celtics were the No. 2 seed in the East.

CHAPTER FIVE

THE 2022 PLAYOFFS

As the second seed, we opened the playoffs with a rematch against the Brooklyn Nets and, of course, Kyrie Irving. The year before our team was falling apart, and the Nets rolled in five easy games, winning by an average of 15 points a game. (Note: Jaylen Brown missed the entire series with a wrist injury.) That was the first year of their superteam with Kevin Durant, James Harden, and Irving as teammates, and they smoked us. The most (in) famous moment in the series was when Irving stomped on the leprechaun logo at midcourt after Game Four.

But this group of Boston Celtics kept receipts. Ime Udoka's squad destroyed them in a four-game sweep that wasn't even that close. Jayson Tatum took this thing over quickly. He dominated, averaging 30 points, five rebounds, and seven assists a game. Most impressively, he dominated K.D., holding the future Hall of Famer to 39 percent shooting and only 33 percent from the three-point line.

The second round was a classic series against the defending champion Milwaukee Bucks and two-time MVP Giannis Antetokounmpo. In the previous year's NBA Finals against the Phoenix Suns, the "Greek Freak" was absolutely epic. Milwaukee was missing All-Star Khris Middleton, but they had some guy named Jrue Holiday along with great role players in Brook Lopez and Bobby Portis. This wasn't going to be easy.

We split the first two games in Boston, and then Antetokounmpo went off in Game Three. The Freak had 42 points, 12 rebounds, and even threw in eight assists, leading the Bucks to a 103–101 win and a 2–1 series lead.

Obviously, Game Four was going to be key. Milwaukee had a four-point lead early in the third quarter, when Antetokounmpo wound up and threw it down over Al Horford and then stared at him, earning a technical. Big Al wasn't thrilled. He just nodded back at him. "That didn't sit well with me," he said. "At that point something switched with me."

Um, yeah it did.

Dirtyard Al got his revenge early in the fourth, trailing by two. After hitting a couple of threes, he got Antetokounmpo to bite on a head fake by the three-point line, took a couple of dribbles, and threw it down in the Freak's face. To add emphasis Horford hit him with a sneaky grown man's elbow that put Antetokounmpo flat on his back. Talk about your Kodak moment. Horford turned into the Incredible Hulk: "You don't want to see me when I'm mad!" He just walked away and flexed to the crowd. This was just ridiculous. On that play Horford was Rocky Balboa going against Ivan Drago in *Rocky IV.* All of the sudden, the Russian was cut, he was bleeding, and his invincibility was gone. That was one of the best scenes of the entire season.

The series was tied 2–2 heading into Game Five, when Antetokounmpo put up 40, and the Bucks then had a chance to close things out at home in Game Six. But Tatum had other ideas.

Antetokounmpo left his heart out on the floor with 44 points and *20 rebounds* to go with six assists. Tatum responded with probably the best game of his career to that point, showing why he was getting mentioned as one of the best players in the league, erupting for 46 points and nine rebounds, absolutely *willing* the series back to Boston.

There was a really sweet moment for me that most people didn't notice. I'd walked up to Tatum many times before games and told him, "You're the baddest motherfucker out here." And he's always kind of just laughed. But at the end of one of the games in the series, he pointed at the crowd and the area where we do the radio broadcast, patted his chest, and pointed to me.

That was one of the coolest things I've had happen as a broadcaster.

Nobody could have ever expected what happened in Game Seven. The Bucks came out on fire, leading by six after the first quarter. That's when Udoka looked down his bench and got the surprise of his life. Grant Williams was a third-year, undersized power forward. He'd battled weight issues early in his career and was now getting some steady minutes. Still, he only scored two points in Game Six. But on this particular Sunday, Williams turned into Larry Bird. He couldn't miss from either corner, hitting seven three-pointers, finishing with 27 points in 39 minutes. The champions were dead, and we were on our way to Miami.

Miami is obviously beautiful. There aren't many places that players look forward to on the road more than South Beach. But the Celtics have never been welcomed there. Since Pat Riley joined the Miami Heat in 1995, we've been public enemy No. 1. Obviously, he had a lot of hate toward us, flashing back to our rivalry in the 1980s. I've never asked Riley, but I'm sure that if you asked him which losses keep him up at night, there's a lot of green in those nightmares.

Two years earlier Jimmy Butler and company had the last laugh, beating us in six games during the Eastern Conference Finals in the bubble. To riff off a famous *Seinfeld* episode, "Playoff Jimmy" was real, and he was spectacular. We came home with a 3–2 series lead. All we had to do was close the Heat out. But Playoff Jimmy had other ideas. He went for 47 points, nine rebounds, and eight assists, sitting out for only two minutes.

We had to head back to South Beach. The boys started out Game Seven on fire, leading by 15 after the first quarter. But one thing that everyone knows about Heat Culture was that that they never go quietly. Butler put Miami on his back; he and Bam Adebayo combined for 60 of the team's 96 points. With 21 seconds to go, we led by two when Marcus Smart missed a tough shot inside, and Butler grabbed the rebound. He went the length of the court and pulled up for the series-winning three-pointer…and front-rimmed it. Brown pulled down the rebound. Smart made two free throws, and the Celtics were back!

People ask what was going through my mind when Butler pulled up. The better question was what was I smelling in my pants? In the last couple of minutes, the Celts missed three three-pointers, going for the home run instead of just hitting singles to put the game away. That was demoralizing. Thank the Lord he missed, and we were going to the Finals!

* * *

The Golden State Warriors had already won three titles. Steph Curry will probably go down as the greatest shooter in NBA history. The backcourt of him and Klay Thompson was just lethal. They'll both be in Springfield once they retire.

Another future Hall of Famer is Draymond Green. An unheralded second-round pick out of Michigan State, Green was critical to the Warriors' success, doing all the dirty work, fighting for rebounds, and guarding the other team's best player. He was even Defensive Player of the Year at one point. By the 2021–22 season, Green was 31 years old, and his offensive game in particular had taken a turn for the worse. He was one of those players you hated if he wasn't on your team. I have the ultimate respect for him and what he does for his squad. But he smelled fresh blood and went after it.

The Celtics won the first game with an incredible 40–16 fourth quarter to complete a huge comeback. Derrick White hit some crazy shots, and a few were in Curry's face. To say Curry was demoralized would be an understatement. The thought of grabbing the first two games on the road was delicious. But just before halftime of Game Two, the series changed.

Golden State led by two, when Jaylen Brown went up for a three-pointer, and was fouled by Green. Draymond being Draymond, he made sure to kick and give Brown a little shove. Then, he taunted the Celtics bench. Our guys had no response, and that told me where this series was heading. The Celtics got punked plain and simple, and I was about to become a story.

On the broadcast I said that if Green had pulled that in the 1980s, he wouldn't have walked out. After the loss I was on the floor, talking with Gary Payton Sr., whose son played for Golden State. Green came over to us and stuck himself in our conversation, talking with Payton. I figured that was a good time to leave and catch the team bus, but Green had other ideas. I noticed that he was walking behind me, following me into the corridor. I turned around and asked him if he had a problem. "Yeah, you said that somebody would hit me." I told him that wasn't accurate, and he responded, "Be about your word. Be about your word."

I then told him what I *had* said, that he wouldn't be coming out of our huddle. Then I added how much I admire what he does for his team. I asked if we were good, and he said we were. We shook hands, and that was the end of it. But it showed me that fire he had in his belly. It also showed me that we didn't have a player who would respond that way and that we'd probably end up losing the series.

Still, the Boston Celtics won Game Three and were in a back-and-forth battle in Game Four. That's when Curry went into Paris mode (like he showed in the 2024 gold medal game) and put it away. In one of the truly phenomenal

Finals performances of all time, he finished with 43 points and 10 rebounds. Unfortunately, that was basically the end of the series. I left there conflicted. Initially, I thought the Celtics were good enough to win a championship, but after this series, I didn't know if they needed something to get over the hump.

Brown's development was the bright spot of the series, as he was our best player. Tatum, on the other hand, went into *his* Paris mode, which was the opposite of Curry's lights-out play.

His shot was off the entire series, which was strange because he entered it playing so well, dominating against guys like Kevin Durant and Giannis Antetokounmpo. But as he struggled, we saw the same type of stuff that happened at the Olympics—drooped shoulders, no confidence, thinking about his shot instead of just playing. He became the first player in league history to have 100 turnovers in a single postseason.

It's no wonder that J.T. had serious doubts about just how good he was. "That was the first time where I thought, *I don't know, maybe I'm not one of the guys that can be the best player on the championship team,*" Tatum said. "It was so hard to get to the Finals, and we still didn't win. Getting there, that was the hardest thing I ever had to do. I was drained. That summer I had moments thinking that maybe you have to be a legend to win a championship. And there were moments where I wondered if I was going to be that guy just because of how hard it is."

After the loss Udoka was looking to the future. "The biggest message was: 'Learn from this, grow from it, take this experience and see there is another level to get to. Just don't come back the same as players, coaching staff. Let this fuel you throughout the offseason into next year,'" he said. "Some guys didn't play their best. That's going to motivate guys throughout the season. The message is: 'Everybody come back better. Let's not be satisfied. It's not guaranteed you're going to be here.'"

It was as if he knew what was about to happen because nobody else could have guessed.

CHAPTER SIX

WAIT...WHAT?!?

It was a normal September day in Boston. The Celtics were rapidly approaching training camp when a bombshell broke—and I *do* mean a bombshell. Ime Udoka was suspended for the 2022–23 season. No further details were given.

Word eventually leaked out that he apparently had an inappropriate relationship with a team employee. I was as shocked as anyone. Reporters were calling me up asking what happened, and I was like, "Dude, I have no idea." Once details started to surface, I was like *whoa*. What really disappointed me was that I *know* this isn't the first time this happened with an NBA coach.

The Boston Globe's Dan Shaughnessy agrees. "I think that it's a tricky one because having covered the league for more than 40 years, that was not a fireable offense over the decades," said Shaughnessy before dropping a bombshell of his own. "I didn't talk to Brad a lot, but when I did, I was really gathering that he wasn't as unhappy to see him go. Not that they didn't like him—I just think they thought they could do better. It was a little bit of a basketball motivation to that. They obviously couldn't let him go based on getting to the Finals. It was one year in the job."

Shaughnessy believed that blowing a 2–1 series lead in the NBA Finals clearly didn't help things, even though Udoka was the NBA Coach of the Month in both February and March.

"There was a sense that year and subsequent months after it that," Shaughnessy said, "they didn't like him as much as a coach as everybody else did. [Brad] really thought Mazzulla would be an upgrade for them. So when you had the behavioral issue, I think it made it easier for them to get real strict on things. Certainly, they honored that with today's ethics."

Bob Ryan didn't get that impression, but he points out that nobody knows what was going on behind closed doors. "We don't have any idea. No one spilled the beans on that one at all, and so we have no idea...whether he was blindsided or whether he was 'I got to deal with this thing now' kind of thing," he said. "We'll never know until we wait for his memoir. But I didn't get that. I have not formed that impression."

Nearly as shocking as Udoka's suspension was the person named to replace him. Let me be honest: I had no idea who Joe Mazzulla was. He was an assistant who didn't even sit in the front row on the bench. It turns out he played at the University of West Virginia for Hall of Fame coach Bob Huggins. Austin Ainge says the organization hired Mazzulla under the category of finding smart people. "We just try to hire very talented people that are dedicated and see how they develop and try to put them in situations to succeed and to help us," he said. "And we had Joe [as an assistant] in Maine initially. I think he made minimum wage or something in our G League with our G League team, and we liked him quite a bit."

From there, Mazzulla went on to become a head coach at Division II Fairmont State University for two years and then came back to the second row of the Celtics' bench. "We hired him back because we did have hopes for him and liked him," Ainge said. "And he was a behind-the-bench assistant for us that we respected and admired and saw something in, but, yeah, certainly we figured he would be a head coach further down the line, but circumstances intervened."

When Udoka came to Boston, one of the big decisions he had to make was the composition of his coaching staff. He met with Mazzulla and kept him on board. "He was a guy that there was a consensus yes," Ainge said, "somebody that [the players] all worked with closely, believed in, and understood his upside."

Mazzulla's background wasn't perfect. In 2009 he was arrested for domestic battery in a bar incident. But he got on the straight and narrow and became a changed man with an incredible focus. "I believe strongly in Joe's substantiveness as a person," Brad Stevens said. "He's been very open with me about how those moments impacted him in every which way, and you can see it in the way he carries himself. He'll be the first to tell you he's 110 percent accountable for that, and I'll be the first to tell you that I believe in him."

Dan Shaughnessy agreed. "He's a beauty," he said. "The fact that he had beat Kentucky as a player [in the NCAA Tournament] was a huge deal. He had his personal transgressions at a young age and cleaned all that up in a magical way where he's such a straight shooter now. I was just interested in him personally and how a young guy got to this position.

I never pay attention to all those assistant coaches. He wasn't even in the front row. [I'd] never heard of him, never noticed him, never knew the name."

I'll say this: Mazzulla is an acquired taste. He's not the guy who's going to make things easy on reporters. Someone may ask him about Black coaches in the league, and Mazzulla will respond, "Are they Christians?" I mean, they're giving you a layup, but he ain't taking that.

Even though this had the feeling of a shotgun marriage, Mazzulla said the abruptness of what happened actually helped him. "I never do well when I have a lot of time to think. That's where I'm not great in some areas. And so the fact that I got the call—*boom*—training camp in four days. It's almost like you go into survival mode," he told JJ Redick on his *The Old Man & the Three* podcast. "You don't have time to think about anything except what's the most important thing right now. It was just like all right…these are the most important things on Day One. We were just doing that. These are the objectives, and so it's almost like you just kind of… don't have time for anything other than figuring out what's most important and going from there. So it actually kind of helped me a little bit in year one. If I went into a situation in year one, and I had to think a lot, I think it would have been a little bit like, 'Do we do this? Do we do that?'"

Even in his short playing/coaching careers, Mazzulla was exposed to coaches who went about things in vastly different ways, which he said gave him the palate to choose what type of coach he wanted to be. "It was a master class working for Brad as an assistant. And then it was another master class working for Ime," he said. "And I got to see two really great coaches, two smart coaches, two people that do it completely different ways, but the principles remain the same."

In college Mazzulla played for two Hall of Famers in John Beilein and Bob Huggins at West Virginia. You would have trouble finding two guys with more different approaches. "But in reality," Mazzulla said, "a lot of the principles and a lot of the concepts that they talked about were the same. They just delivered the message differently and built relationships with the players differently. And so when I got the job, I had one of the greatest gifts. I saw it go one way, be really successful. I saw it be really successful another way. I can take from both of them because they're an influence on my coaching career."

Here's an example of why I like Mazzulla so much. The team does various events for sponsors and fans, and on one occasion, I was the resident pro who was going to come in, tell stories, sign autographs, take pictures, etc. I stayed a little longer on this particular day, and I saw Joe just walking around the empty court. He did about five laps. I noticed that he's rubbing his rosary beads in his hands. He wasn't really saying anything, just rubbing those beads. After his second lap, he stopped where I was at. We hadn't spoken too much up to that point, but obviously we knew who each other was. Mazzulla looked up at our championship banners and asked me which ones I won. (He knew I was the Finals MVP in 1981 but didn't know my other year.) I shared that we beat the Los Angeles Lakers for the 1984 title, and he looked me dead in the eyes and told me, "I will do anything to get a banner up there. I'll do *anything.*"

Mazzulla literally was on the verge of tears. I remember thinking, *This fucking guy is serious. He is on a mission.* I turned to Mazzulla and told him not to cry, just get it done. Without hesitation Mazzulla looked at me and said, "We're gonna get this thing done."

Mazzulla has a slightly different memory of our meeting. "I wasn't *on the verge* of tears," he said. "I was crying."

The way Mazzulla almost reveres those who have come before him is something I obviously really dig. "I have an innate respect and appreciation for you," he told me. "[You're] a Finals MVP, and you walk around the organization like you're just another guy," he said. "And to me that represents what being a Celtic is about. It's bigger than you. It's about the team. It's about the tradition, it's about winning."

Mazzulla said his walk puts his mind at ease. "It's daily," he said. "I do it at the garden and I spend a lot of time thanking and praying and I thank God really for the pressures of the job. I thank him for the anxiety, I thank him for the difficulties, I thank him for the opportunity."

Stevens knew Coach Mazzulla would make the most of this opportunity. "He's an outstanding leader. I think he's done a great job right from the get-go of galvanizing our locker room around a mission," he said. "I know he gives a damn about everybody in that locker room. He really, really cares. It eats him up when something doesn't go well individually for a guy. It eats him up when he feels like he's let the team down."

Players like Derrick White instantly saw Mazzulla's commitment to them. "Man, I love Joe Mazzulla so much," White said, "Coming off the year I had, and he gets the job, and he's like, 'You know what? I'm going to start you,' which I wasn't expecting. He was like, 'I believe in you, and I trust in you. This is going to give you the confidence.' And from that moment on, I think it's changed my whole career. I'd do anything for him."

I think we have to give Stevens and the front office credit. Think about it: the team goes to the Finals, then just before training camp, they lose their coach. Stevens made a bold decision, hiring a virtual unknown, but was absolutely resolute in that call. "Joe is the best choice to [take over] by a long shot," Stevens said. "He's an exceptionally sharp and talented person. I believe strongly in him and his ability to lead people, his ability to galvanize a room and get behind them, and his ability to organize and understand all that comes with running a team during a season."

Tatum also vouched for Mazzulla. "We don't know what the belief and faith in him and confidence in him was internally. When it all came down, the first person of consequence who offered a public endorsement of Joe Mazzulla was Jayson Tatum," Ryan said. "He came right out and said, 'Oh, this is good, Joe Mazzulla.' He said very positive things about him, which was a good indication. It struck me right away. I said, 'Oh, that's good. This player is okay with this, and he's going out of his way—absolutely out of his way—to endorse something.' So I think they have faith in what we can tell in both those guys.

"I'm forever grateful to that group of guys, Jaylen and Jayson in particular, giving me a chance. They didn't have to, but their character, who they are as people, who they are as players, they allow me to be a good coach. And that's the greatest gift any coach could have is high-character talent, allowing you to coach them."

Mazzulla was the right guy at the right time, and he definitely understood what he was walking into. And he made sure to follow Stevens' lead. "Everybody sets the temperature when they come in. Brad, giving me my start, hiring me, empowering me from Day One as an assistant, and giving me some of the opportunities that he has," Mazzulla said, "but also the way he carries himself. I've always had a lot of respect for how he went about coaching, how he kept family balance No. 1, how he treated people No. 1. That was always more important than whether there was a success or a failure. I think he spearheads the leadership, the temperature of the building, just as everybody else does."

CHAPTER SEVEN

JOE'S FIRST DANCE

L osing your coach just before training camp can be discombobulating enough, but the Boston Celtics now had their *third* head coach in four years. Compare that to the nine years of Doc Rivers, and it was very unsettling. But Joe Mazzulla had the absolute belief in himself, which made things a little easier.

Austin Ainge was in awe of his new coach. "It was an underreported story that he walked in, and we were just lights out," he said. "We were playing unbelievable. I really can't say more good things about Joe and obviously his staff who had some holdovers and people that Joe was promoted over. They had to swallow their egos and join in and then obviously always the players."

Mazzulla had built a relationship with his guys, even as a back bench assistant. Your best players having your back is always important—especially in a strange situation like this. "I'm forever grateful to that group of guys, Jaylen and Jayson in particular, giving me a chance," he said. "They didn't have to, but their character, who they are as people, who they are as players, they allow me to be a good coach. And that's the greatest gift any coach could have is high character talent, allowing you to coach them. And I'm forever grateful for that."

Mazzulla was treating his new job like a triage unit, taking it one step at a time. "I wasn't definitely like, 'Oh, I got this all figured out.' I was like, 'Okay, this is gonna be really hard," he told JJ Redick on his podcast. "But I tried not to think too far ahead. I was just like, 'I'm only gonna worry about now 'til training camp ends. And then when training camp ends, we'll just figure out the first 20 games. And then we'll see what happens.'"

What happened was that the team took off, winning 20 of its first 25 games. The Jays were playing the best ball of their careers. Jayson Tatum was on his way to his second straight first team All-NBA recognition, while Jaylen Brown made his second All-Star team. Things went so well that Mazzulla ended up coaching the All-Star game (in his first season as head coach) and watched Tatum drop 55 points en route to the game's MVP award.

It was surreal to watch how the guys were playing, knocking down shots, and playing almost in a college-like way.

We were all learning about Mazzulla, but even though I didn't know much about him, I shouldn't have been surprised. Ime Udoka and his staff would always play half-court basketball before their games. You'd think these would feature older guys, guys going like half-speed. You'd be wrong. This was like Celtics–Lakers from the 1980s! These guys were taking people out. You'd see Mazzulla going through a pick and doing it with a forearm shiver. A couple of coaches even had black eyes; their lips were bloody! Who plays like that with assistant coaches? The first few times I saw them play, I thought it was cute. Then, I was like, *Oh, they play like this all the time.* It was like roller derby. That opened up my eyes to who Joe Mazzulla was.

Brad Stevens wasn't wasting time in improving the roster either. His first trade was Kemba Walker to the Oklahoma City Thunder for Al Horford, who had left two years earlier.

The question was what did Horford actually have left? Horford had left to sign a four-year, $109 million deal with the Philadelphia 76ers, which, to be polite, was a disaster. His numbers with the Sixers weren't awful, but, as he told *Sports Illustrated*, things just didn't work playing next to Joel Embiid. "I just think it just wasn't a good fit. We just weren't jelling. We weren't meshing. And obviously we had a lot of big guys out there in particular out playing, and it just wasn't fitting," he said. "[It] was frustrating because I could never really show what I was capable of or play my game…I've always known that I'm able to play. I know that I can play at a high level. That's never been an issue for me."

Things went so poorly that the Sixers dumped him and his salary on Oklahoma City. Playing with the young guys on the Thunder, Big Al rediscovered his love of the game, and then the tanking team didn't play him over the last part of the season so they'd get a better draft pick.

Still, when Big Al looks back on his trials, he said it was a positive. "It was great to have that," he said. "It was an exciting time for me to go through all that. Right away, I'm thinking ahead about everything we need to do."

Make no mistake, though, Horford was glad to be wearing green again. "I'm really, really happy to be back," he said. "I really appreciate how special of a place Boston is. Being away, I know how special the city is and how special the team is to the city."

Though Horford and the rest of the guys were playing well for Mazzulla in his first season, there were some concerns that people would bring up. Personally, I'd covered the Jays for their entire career but had never really seen them play *together*. It was like they were coworkers, but you didn't see them chest bump or act excited for each other. They were both out there doing their jobs. With Tatum as the linchpin for the offense, much of what the team did was centered around him, but Brown had his moments as well.

There were also some quirks with Mazzulla. The most notable one was that he *never* called timeouts. The other was that he believed when the three-ball wasn't going down, the team should shoot *more* of them. As a post player, that was difficult for me to wrap my head around.

In Mazzulla's first playoff go-around, the team started by playing the Atlanta Hawks.

Going back to my days, the Hawks have always been that thorn-in-your-side for us. Hell, I remember when Tree Rollins *actually* bit Danny Ainge one year—and Ainge got blamed for it!

Atlanta guard Trae Young tore us up, averaging 29 points per game. Somehow, the Hawks, who were 41–41 on the season, gave us a good battle, but we won in six games.

A familiar foe was next—the Sixers and league MVP Joel Embiid. The big man missed the first game, so naturally Philadelphia won in Boston, as James Harden went for 45 points.

Weirdly, Embiid returned in Game Two. Yet, the Celtics won by 34 points. The series went back and forth, and we went back to Philadelphia, needing to win Game Six to stay alive. Fortunately, we got some help, as Harden went 4-of-16 from the floor (0-for-6 from downtown) to finish with 13 points and five turnovers. It was really fascinating to watch Harden shrivel up.

Back in 2011 Danny Ainge made a trade to get Jeff Green from Oklahoma City, but the guy he really wanted was Harden. To see how well he played to start this series before basically vanishing was stunning. The Celtics didn't change the gameplan. He just imploded. You couldn't help but think about what would have happened if the trade had gone through. I mean, "the Beard" was such a great scorer. He probably would have been the greatest pure scorer in Celtics history. But his play in the clutch? Well...Anyway, for some reason, they decided not to give the ball to Embiid down the stretch of Game Six, and we eked out a 95–86 win.

It was like a flashback to the days when we played at the Spectrum with the passion of the fans and more importantly their disappointment when we beat them. Good times indeed!

Remember how I'd told Tatum that he was the baddest motherfucker in the league? Well, he showed it in Game Seven at home. From the beginning of the game, he was putting his statement out there. It was like Tatum was telling the Sixers, "This is who I am. I'm Jayson Tatum, and you're Gumby." Tatum just imposed his will in every facet of the game from beginning to end. He played with the same swagger I saw him show Kevin Durant the year before. I mean, this was incredible: 17-of-28 from the floor and six three-pointers for 51 points! He threw in 13 rebounds and five assists...and no turnovers. Brown added 25 of his own, and the Celtics won by 24 points.

There was no way our old friend Doc Rivers was going to survive this one, especially after Harden threw him under the bus. That Philly fan base is something else. They are just fanatics. I always say they're the best winners, but also the best losers, LOL. Meanwhile, we were ready for Miami—again.

CHAPTER EIGHT

CRASH LANDING

The Miami Heat weren't even supposed to *be* in the Eastern Conference Finals. They had only won 44 games during the season. They actually lost the first play-in game to the Atlanta Hawks, but you can never count Erik Spoelstra out. After escaping the Hawks, Miami shocked the Milwaukee Bucks, who were playing with a wounded Giannis Antetokounmpo, and then upset the New York Knicks in six.

They were hot, but we *did* win 13 more games than Miami. I knew we were the better team, but someone forgot to tell the Heat. For years the Boston Celtics had "Playoff Rondo," where Rajon Rondo would be a completely different player in the postseason. The Heat had "Playoff Jimmy." Jimmy Butler will go to the Hall of Fame, but sometimes I think he gets bored in the regular season. That's not the case in the play-offs. Some guys (including yours truly), we just go to another gear. It's not really like we're coasting during the season, but it's just an extra kick in the playoffs, and it knocks people off balance. The fact that Jimmy always has something to say makes you dislike him even that much more as a player, but I'm telling you: he's like Clark Kent, going into a phone booth and coming out as Superman.

In Game One of the 2023 Eastern Conference Finals, the Celtics were up by nine at halftime. Then came the third quarter. Over the next 12 minutes, Butler dropped 12 points, Max Strus—*Max Strus?*—had 13, and Bam Adebayo had nine. The Heat dominated, outscoring us 46–25. Butler punched the Celtics, and we never recovered.

Game Two followed a similar script. This time, the Celts led by eight going into the fourth quarter...only to lose by six en route to falling behind 2–0 at home. Butler had 27 points in this one, and Caleb Martin and his 9.8-points-per-game average dropped 25. There wasn't much drama in Game Three. Miami led by 15 at half, and by 30 after three. The Jays were awful; they went 12 for 35 from the floor and only 1-of-14 from the three-point line. Joe Mazzulla's "shoot three until you drop" theory didn't work, as the team dropped only 26 percent of their shots from behind the arc. And the Heat could do no wrong. "That was a solid, mature, professional approach," Spoelstra said. "There's a lot of pent-up stuff here, and we're getting closer, but we still have to finish this off."

That's the thing with the Heat. They've always had the ability to get under our skin. As an analyst I see things a bit different than fans. I see the ebbs and flows, and it's almost like seeing the future when you watch the game. The Heat weren't as good as the Celtics, but they always had a little something else they wanted to dig at you. They would muddy the game up to make up for the skill discrepancy, and the games would always be ugly. When Miami won a game in 2024, I passed Coach Spoelstra and said, "Nice game, Coach."

He thanked me. Then I added, "Well, I really didn't mean it."

He said, "I know."

This vibe even goes through the broadcasters. Heat play-by-play voice Jason Jackson and I always give it to each other when we play. We do it in fun, but there are times where I feel like a player again. When we go up against them or the Los Angeles Lakers, those games are personal. And through three games, Miami looked like a team while we were coming up short.

"To their credit they're playing well above their means," Jaylen Brown said. "They're ballin' right now, and I've got to give them respect. Gabe Vincent, Martin, Strus, Duncan Robinson, guys that we should be able to keep under control, are playing their [butts] off."

The series was 3–0, and it looked like the series was over. It sure sounded like it in the Celtics locker room. "I don't even know where to start," Brown said. "It's an obvious letdown. I feel like we let our fanbase, organization down. We let ourselves down. And it was collective. We can point fingers. But in reality it's just embarrassing."

"I just didn't have them ready to play," Mazzulla said. "I have to get them in a better place to be ready to play, and that's on me."

Tatum sounded like a beaten man. "We've got to have some pride, bounce back, and just be better come Tuesday," he said.

But leave it to Al Horford to give perspective. He was in his 16th season and desperately wanted a ring. "We're not out yet," Horford said. "It is 3–0. I know what it looks like. [But] we're not out yet. We're still kicking. One of four teams that are still kicking."

I vividly remember the day of Game Four. Mazzulla decided not to have a shootaround that morning. So all the guys were out, hanging by the pool. They all seemed to be very, very focused. It wasn't like doom and gloom, guys were talking, laughing, but this was clearly the calm before the storm. Marcus Smart was the leader. He had a "I don't give a damn, we ain't losing" attitude, and that's how everyone played.

The guys bounced back. Tatum had 33 points, 11 rebounds, and seven assists. This time it was the Celtics who erupted in the third quarter, staying alive with a 38–23 stretch. Home cooking was what the Celtics needed for Game Five, as the Jays, Derrick White, and Smart all scored more than 20 points in an easy win. That set the stage for one of the most memorable moments in Celtics playoff history.

Game Six in Miami—hostile crowd, house of horrors, and needing a win to stay alive—that's what the team was facing. But one thing we've learned about this group is that they are road warriors. Nothing intimidates them. It was a back-and-forth game, and I was cautiously optimistic as we held a seven-point lead going into the fourth quarter. Tatum wasn't shooting great but had 25 through three periods and was pounding the boards. You look at the box score, and you see Butler went 5-of-21 from the floor. But if you watched the game, "Playoff Jimmy" did his Kobe Bryant, Game Seven imitation from 2010, scoring 15 points, including eight from the free-throw line. Things were falling apart for the Green. "I don't know if poise is a great word to use with those last four minutes," White said, laughing after the game, "but we found a way to win."

White willed them to a one-point lead with three seconds left. All season long there were questions about who would take the big shot at the most important moment. We had All-NBA Tatum and All-Star Brown. So with the season on the line, who took the shot? Marcus Smart.

He missed it, but D-White came out of nowhere for the biggest putback in Celtics history. It even faked out the TNT announcers, who thought the shot was too late.

But it wasn't.

Funny thing is that if White didn't make the play, you know Smart would have been *killed* for taking the shot. If that happened, I still would have given Smart huge props for taking it. Not like he was the best shooter on the team, but he wasn't afraid of the moment. The good news is White did make the play, and we were going back home for Game Seven on the cusp of becoming the only team in league history to complete a comeback from three games down.

* * *

The list of teams in sports history who have come back from a 3–0 series is short, starting with one that all Boston fans know about: the Red Sox beating the New York Yankees in the 2004 American League Championship Series. There aren't a lot more.

1942—Toronto Maple Leafs defeat the Detroit Red Wings in the Stanley Cup Finals

1975—New York Islanders defeat the Philadelphia Flyers
in Stanley Cup Playoffs

I was convinced that the Celtics were going to be the
first NBA team to ever climb that mountain. Derrick White's
tip-in had to have broken the Miami Heat's spirit, right? And
the game was in Boston. So there's no way we're going to
lose that one. I was *positive* they were going to win. If, if, if
I was ever going to bet on a game—and no, Commissioner
Silver, I *don't bet*—but if I did, this would have been the one.
Normally, when you take a team's best shot and essentially
ride them down, that dogs them like that, and it's over.

But in the first minute, Jayson Tatum got the ball on the
right wing, pump faked Caleb Martin, drove to the basket,
took it to the hole on the closing Gabe Vincent, drew a
blocking foul...and turned his left ankle. Game. Over.

Talk about the air going out of the building. If people
don't realize how big a deal that was, they don't know basketball. I give Tatum credit. He really gutted it out, playing more
than 41 minutes on that ankle, but he had no lift, no elevation.
He crawled to the finish line of this one, missing eight of his
13 shots, though he did somehow grab 11 rebounds. But his
injury was like Pigpen with Charlie Brown. You know the
guy who walks around with a cloud of dirt following him?
Once J.T. got hurt, there was dirt all over the place.

The game, as you can imagine, was never close. We'd lost
our main weapon, and Jaylen Brown was just 8-of-23 from
the floor (1-of-9 from three) and had *eight* turnovers. "We
failed. I failed. We let the whole city down. He couldn't move

out there. It was tough for him," Brown said of Tatum. "And my team turned to me to make plays and etc., and I came up short. I failed. And it's tough. I give credit to Miami but just a terrible job."

At halftime Charles Barkley, who had guaranteed a Boston Celtics win, put it pretty bluntly. "Watching these dumbass Celtics play is making my head hurt. It's so bad to watch them play," Barkley said. "There's no ball movement. There's no body movement, and it's just frustrating watching a team with this much talent just play stupid."

As usual, Chuck wasn't shy with his opinion. Having said that, I can't say enough about Brown after this series. Here's a guy, who (after being named All-NBA) was about to get the biggest contract in the NBA worth more than $300 million, and he sat there, taking this loss like a man. The Brown we saw a year later was more of a finished product; this Brown hadn't flexed his muscles yet.

Derrick White was still finding his way with this group, and Marcus Smart was not a factor. The Heat won 103–84 and were going to the NBA Finals. In his postgame news conference, Brad Stevens tried to sound optimistic. "There was a lot that went right," he said. "And we can't lose sight of that."

He mentioned making "small tweaks" to the roster. Maybe he wrote that in pencil because instead of minor tweaks, the Celtics were about to undergo a major roster overhaul.

CHAPTER NINE

WHEELING AND DEALING

The days after losing to the Miami Heat—heck, even during that series—there was more talk than ever about breaking up the Jays. Jayson Tatum and Jaylen Brown had been together for six seasons. They'd done almost everything, gone to multiple Eastern Conference Finals, even made it to the NBA Finals, but they kept coming up short of their goal. Tatum was first-team All-NBA again, and Brown made second team for the first time. At least Tatum had an excuse vs. the Heat: he was hurt. Brown had no shelter. "You take it on the chin. You learn from it," Brown said. "As hard as this one is to swallow, you get better. Tough one, tough one, tough one for me. Tough one for our team. Tough one for our organization. Extremely bad timing, you just learn. And it's part of the journey. This is not the end. We got a lot better to get, a lot of better basketball to play. And you just got to look at it like that but tough night."

By virtue of his All-NBA honor, Brown was eligible for a supermax contract, which would be the highest salary in league history. But would that happen in Boston? There were several "experts" who thought the team had reached its ceiling. "The Jays were too similar," they said. "You can't build a team around two wings."

One of the most interesting things is that while so many fans thought of the season as a failure, that wasn't the case with management, and Austin Ainge said there was no inter-est in breaking up this team. "We talk about everything, but nothing was ever seriously contemplated. I mean, we cer-tainly have the opposite view in that this is unprecedented, amazing success, not that this was failure, right?" Ainge said. "Through age 25 the success that those guys had, we knew that their primes were still coming up. So we did not view this as some big failure of their early part of their career, the exact opposite. We were amazed at the success. I mean, most teams, ownerships, front offices, coaching staffs would die, would celebrate the success that those guys had. So even though we didn't win the title at that point, we were aware of how much success that is and how hard it is to win and get to that point, and we did not take that for granted."

Bob Ryan remembers his podcast cohost, Jeff Goodman, wasn't so sure about Brown specifically. "Jeff was determined to trade him for Bradley Beal. He wanted Beal desperately, and I think he was willing to trade Jaylen Brown to get him, I'll put it that way," Ryan said before acknowledging some issues he saw as well. "The biggest problem was [Brown's] dribbling into traffic and his weakness going to his left and dribbling into traffic and at times and coming out without the ball way too much. Other than that I wasn't unhappy with the overall idea of Jaylen Brown. I was very happy to have him."

Some media members, well, let's say they didn't agree. "It's time to break Jaylen Brown and Jayson Tatum up," said former Boston Celtics big man Kendrick Perkins, who's now an ESPN studio analyst, after Game Seven. "If you're the front office of the Celtics, I just don't know how much longer you're going to be patient with this duo."

Then he dropped a haymaker. "The front office, Brad Stevens, and Wyc Grousbeck is gonna have to take a hard look at whether they want to bring Jaylen Brown back and pair him up with Jayson Tatum," Perkins said. "They should go out and get a Damian Lillard, and if they fall short, they should try and get a Trae Young. But I think it's time to end this relationship right now."

This might be a good time for all Celtics fans to be thankful that Perk isn't running the team.

I thought there was still room to grow, but there were some definite shortcomings. The biggest was they needed some scoring in the paint. Rob Williams was a really good defender and great at catching lobs, but competing on the offensive end wasn't in his skillset. The bigger issue for Williams has always been health. He's only played 60 games in one season. That's not his fault, but it's a major factor.

We were a really good team but couldn't get over the hump. Not everyone thought we had to shake things up. "I'll tell you what I said at the time. It's not about talent," Ryan said. "They do not need a major talent infusion." That doesn't mean we didn't have holes, which Ryan noted. "I always thought they could use another pure shooter at the time, and rebounding was occasionally an issue."

Whatever issues there were, we know that Brad Stevens doesn't waste any time when making his moves. It took less than a month for him to dramatically reshape the team in a single move, and it wasn't an easy one. Stevens said he keeps a list of 20-to-30 guys that he would investigate if they became available. He knew that the Washington Wizards were going nowhere, and Kristaps Porzingis had a player option, so there might be something there. The Celtics and Wizards talked for about a week, at which point Stevens knew he was gettable. The next step was assessing the cost.

He worked out a three-way trade with the Memphis Grizzlies and Washington, sending Marcus Smart to the Grizzlies, getting Porzingis in return, and somehow picking up two first-round picks in the deal. Stevens said he wouldn't have given up as valuable a player as Smart if Derrick White hadn't begun to emerge as such a key piece. He wasn't a replacement, but he was an integral part of the team moving forward. "Derrick is an outstanding player, and you can see that his comfort level—he felt so much more comfortable this year," Stevens explained. "It's not comparing one against the other or whatever the case. It's just the way that this deal materialized and the way that it gave us an opportunity to balance our roster. As heart-wrenching as it was to part with Marcus is, [it's] something what we felt like we had to do. We're going need Derek to continue to be great, and we have no doubt that he will."

I had many thoughts when I heard about the deal. Porzingis obviously had talent, but to be honest, I looked at him as a losing player. This was a guy who had been in the league eight seasons, including one he missed after tearing his ACL, and had played in only *13* playoff games. To contrast that Brown had been around for seven years and had been in *112*.

Porzingis also had a huge injury history, having only appeared in more than 60 games three times. Ainge was well aware. "The injury concerns are real with his history, but we had seen real, real growth from Kristaps in Washington, and he was obviously very talented," Ainge said. "We had just seen growth in his game. He's really worked hard and developed. We kept watching and watching and saw an opportunity to improve the talent of our group and thought he really did that."

But early in his career, when Porzingis went up against us, Stevens would put Smart on him. K.P. had an 11-inch height advantage, and you know what? Smart would drive his ass crazy.

Smart was that Swiss Army knife player, and if you were out in the damn woods, you'd want him by your side. He was like MacGyver, a crafty guy who would make shit happen.

When I asked Stevens about what he was thinking, he said, "When Porzingis played with Washington the year before, he dropped 32 on us." (That was actually his last game of the season, as the tanking Wizards rested him the last six games). Stevens' vision was that K.P. could be a real weapon on a good team. "He has just gotten better and better and better," Stevens said when announcing the deal. "You see what he was doing this year, and I thought in the games that we played against him, he's already good, but he just took another step, and he can play defensively the way we want to. He is a deterrent at the rim. And he's a super skilled basketball player. We didn't post a ton this year, but to be able to throw the ball in the post and just shoot over a switch and do it so efficiently and effectively is a big deal—let alone be able to play behind the line, shoot the ball, or drive it, or those type of things…You can envision, as I can envision, kind of some of the lineups we can put out there size-wise right now. Pretty intriguing and not without dropping any skill at all. So that's a good thing."

Truth be told, I still wasn't totally sold. Porzingis was pretty much in the witness protection program after leaving the New York Knicks; his Dallas stop didn't work out. He couldn't make it fit with one of the best players in the world—Mavericks guard Luka Doncic. So how would he mesh with the two Jays?

To his credit, K.P. now admits that communication and maturity with him and Doncic could have been better. He also points out that the Mavs were heavy into analytics maybe sooner than most teams, and he wasn't ready for that. "At that stage of my career, [they could have] presented to me the right way and said, 'This is what we need you to do and this is what we need from you. This is the way you're going to be more effective,'" K.P. recalled on *The Old Man & The Three* podcast with JJ Redick. "Kind of explain it to me better. I think that would have made a difference a little bit…but I could have done some things better, and it didn't come out the way like all of us envisioned…definitely learned a lot from that."

In addition to the Celtics' dependence on analytics, that could be a problem, but Stevens wasn't worried. "I know that he is extremely team oriented, extremely excited to be here… This is an accomplished team that he's joining, and he wants

86

to help," Stevens said. "So you can't expect somebody to come in yelling and loud and vocal. And sometimes it's better to come in and just figure out how you can help and add value in the way that you feel most comfortable in your skin. And I'm sure he'll do that."

After the failed experiment in Dallas, Porzingis spent a year and a half in Washington. He played well, but like I said, this was like a tree falling in the woods, and his one-and-a-half years in Washington, well, let's just say he wasn't exactly on the big stage. "Who pays attention to the Wizards?" said Ryan, who then researched that he had averaged 23 points a game with the Wizards. "And I learned that some of it actually was posting up, that he was utilizing that ability, too. And I didn't realize how good an overall defender he was, not just protecting the rim, but he had a lot better mobility than I knew. I wasn't a big fan of his. I said, 'Okay, we'll see.'"

Ryan's compatriot on *The Boston Globe*, Dan Shaughnessy, felt the same way. "I was like, 'Oh yeah, I forgot about him.' When he came out with the Knicks, he was the next big thing. The notion of having him on your team was, I think, it was almost like the way it was with you when Giannis became everybody's big deal," Shaughnessy said. "I know he kept getting hurt and didn't win. I couldn't have told you I know he's with Washington at the end."

There was one other thing. For this deal to happen, K.P. would have to opt into his contract. Seeing the salary explosion in the NBA, he definitely would be leaving some money on the table. For Porzingis that didn't matter. "I wanted to be challenged," he said. "My last year in Dallas, the year before

I got traded, I didn't have the best playoff series. We got kicked out in the first round. And now I'm like, 'Okay, I have to prove to everybody that I can play on a playoff or championship caliber team and perform, remind everybody that can happen.'"

Interestingly enough, it was playing for the woeful Wizards that reignited the spark for K.P., as he told ESPN. "What I always wanted is to win at the biggest stage. A lot of times I was frustrated because I never got that rhythm that I really wanted," he said. "Once I got traded from Dallas to Washington, I feel like I got that joy back. I got that rhythm back. And now I get the opportunity to showcase that talent and hopefully that rhythm that I've been searching for so long."

Charles Barkley said after the deal that you can be a great scorer on a really bad team. Was Porzingis just a guy putting up numbers in games that didn't matter? We'd find out soon enough.

* * *

The other part of the Kristaps Porzingis deal just tore me up: losing Marcus Smart.

I'm not going to say Smart leaving brought tears to my eyes, but I can say I was nearly as devastated as he was. Let me put it this way: I'd chop of one of my fingers to play with Smart. That's how much I love him as a player. Just take the tip of my pinkie, okay? Do a Ronnie Lott. No problem, I'll just have four fingers. Maybe I won't be able to use a rotary phone but no problem.

Here's the bottom line—when he was in the starting lineup, we had our best chance to win. In many ways he was the heartbeat of the team and not afraid to speak his mind. Just think back to the Chicago Bulls game when he called out the Jays for not wanting to pass. On the court I 100 percent believe that he's the best non-center defender the Celtics have *ever* had. And that includes my guy, Dennis Johnson, who's in the Hall of Fame.

I was definitely in the minority, but I thought the group of Jayson Tatum, Jaylen Brown, Rob and Grant Williams, and Smart still had room to grow. The loss to the Miami Heat was devastating, but it was Smart who brought the team back from down 3–0. There's no doubt Smart was a polarizing player; whatever he did was either the greatest or dumbest thing ever. Ime Udoka told me that he would allow Smart one "oh shit" shot per game. In other words, he knew that Smart would take one crazy shot, but for him to be himself, we just had to accept it.

Not everyone, though, agreed with my take on Smart. "You can't keep going back with the same cast, and they didn't. Smart was the one that was extracted," *The Boston Globe*'s Dan Shaughnessy said. "I mean, the Williams boys as well, but it was really the Smart extracting that was the seismic move for Stevens to make. It just felt like you can't keep coming back to the same old, same old, and this is their time."

Even while Shaughnessy saw Smart's value, he felt like there were too many cooks in the kitchen. "I know that Smart was always on the floor at the end of games, and I felt that he was the kind of player that Red would have really liked a lot, and that kind of kept me invested in him a little bit," he said. "It was that whole thing about taking too many shots at the end. You know that's the reason you're open. He needed too much to be, to make it a threesome, and be the alpha dog. He had to be part of a three, but it was really a two and one."

But losing Smart still hurt. Even against the Heat, people remember Derrick White's incredible putback at the buzzer to win Game Six in Miami. It was an all-time Celtics shot, but a lot of fans were pissed that Smart missed the shot that led to it, asking why he'd take it with the season on the line instead of one of the Jays. But I saw it as if there's one player on that team who was never intimidated by the moment, it was Marcus Smart.

I remember being in an elevator in Orlando with Smart. This was just around the time we started to play well for Udoka. The team had decided to make him the point guard, and things were definitely heading in the right direction. So we were heading down in the airport, and I said something about how well he and the team were playing. I'll never forget his response for as long as I live. Smart looked me dead in the eye and said, "That's what happens when you let your fucking point guard handle the basketball!"

Not knowing how the new-look Celtics would play with Porzingis, I was just so torn. Smart was essentially the alarm system that was on your house. It's like if the Boston Celtics lived in a bad neighborhood and had just gotten rid of their pit bull and Ring camera. Who was going to do that for the team?

Austin Ainge remembers saying goodbye to a guy who bled green for nine up-and-down years. "Everybody loves Marcus, and he was hard to move because he's one of all of our favorite guys and players, but we just thought we needed to balance our roster a little bit," he said. "Derrick had been playing so well. We knew he could step up with a bigger role. We saw that Kristaps would take us to a different place and open up different schemes and lineups that we could use against bigger teams. So we thought it would give us a better chance to win."

When they announced the trade, Brad Stevens was clearly emotional talking about Smart, calling it "really hard." "I said this at the start of the summer: I thought that we needed to balance our roster and make sure that we looked at the best ways to do that," he told NBC Sports Boston. "That meant that we were going to likely lose a really, really, really good player...I would say that every time you make calls like that you're probably shaving years off your own career. It's been a pleasure to watch him grow from his first couple days in and out of Boston to what he became as a player. He was always a great teammate, always was a person that you know gave of himself for the team, and really, I thought, grew a lot as a player and will continue to."

About three months after the deal, Smart got married, and this shows you how tight the team is. Among his wedding guests were Tatum, Brown, Grant Williams, and...the guy who traded him—Stevens! What do you get a guy who you just traded?

* * *

It was the summer of 2023, and Brad Stevens had already confirmed his status as someone who wasn't afraid to wheel and deal, but I thought this team was still a little short even after dealing for Kristaps Porzingis. Stevens, though, said he actually was prepared to stand pat. "I thought we were really, really good because we still had Malcolm Brogdon and Rob Williams," Stevens said. "Those guys were both going to be healthy and ready for the start of the season, and we were going to go into the season with what I thought was a really deep team that had a lot of different answers."

Austin Ainge says management knew the trade was no guarantee. "We thought we were really good before we made the Kristaps trade," he said. "We'd had many years in contention, and so, yeah, it's always scary to make a change when you're already very good, right? It's risky because you could get worse. But we thought it was a good risk to take with K.P."

The Milwaukee Bucks were another team, which was trying to get better. Giannis Antetokounmpo was entering the final year of his contract, and the Bucks had gone from winning the title to losing to us in the conference semis to a stunning five-game loss in the first round to the Miami Heat. Their front office knew they had to do something to make Antetokounmpo happy.

Damian Lillard was the greatest player in Portland Trail Blazers history, but he felt like he'd never had a true shot to win a title. At 32 years old, the future Hall of Famer knew his time was winding down, and the Trail Blazers were in the middle of a full rebuild. There was no question where Dame wanted to go. He desperately yearned to play for the Heat, and his agent did everything he could to make it happen. But at the end of the day, the Bucks were apparently more desperate and decided to go for it. It was a three-team deal. Milwaukee sent Grayson Allen to the Phoenix Suns and Jrue Holiday in addition to swapping first-round picks with the Portland Trail Blazers. In exchange they got Lillard and *no* financial flexibility.

This was a star-for-star, bona fide blockbuster deal, and to say it took Holiday by surprise would be an insult to surprises. "In the offseason you go in. I'm already in Milwaukee because my kids go to school there, and they started school, and we working out. I mean, most of the team is there working out. Monday, Tuesday, I work out. I take Wednesday off, kind of do my own thing. Recovery day," he told Draymond Green on his podcast. "I'm taking a nap and I got my watch on, my Apple watch on, and I see the text. I see a call from GM, and I'm like, 'I'll call him back,' like I'm deep in this nap, too. I'm saying it's a good one. And then two seconds later, my agent calls me. I'm like, 'All right.' So I pick up this call. He's, 'Well, you just got traded. So you should probably call him back.' And then I ended up looking at my phone. He ended up texting me everything that was happening…Just like the world had no clue, I also had no clue."

Everyone around the league knew that Holiday wasn't long for Portland. A team starting over wouldn't want a 33-year-old guard making more than $35 million. The race was on. The Heat, Los Angeles Clippers, and Philadelphia

76ers were reportedly interested in Holiday. He was essentially a man without a team but was grateful that the Blazers sent him to a contending team. "I'm in limbo for three days, like not really knowing what's going on, and then when it all kind of came together at the end, I mean, I really thank God for Portland and Chauncey and the GM there because they really did good by me," he said, "just really asking me and talking to me where I wanted to go."

Austin Ainge remembers that the trade talks progressed pretty fast. "I know we had conversations very quickly," he said. "Portland was having discussions with multiple teams very quickly. The whole league knew it wasn't a long-term thing. So we were, yeah, we had very quick discussions."

Stevens told NBC Sports Boston that even back during his coaching days that he'd always ask Danny Ainge if Holiday was available. That desire manifested itself in being ready to pull the trigger. "The good news is you're in touch with a lot of these people all year round, and so just to maintain contact, there certainly were several communications long before this became available," he said. "You do start doing the math on, 'Hey, if Lillard gets traded somewhere other than Miami, there might be contracts that have to be traded and moved to make it work.' And if those happen, then will Portland keep them based on where they are? And I knew [Blazers GM Joe Cronin] liked our guys, and so we were talking pretty quickly. But it's one of those things: there's a lot of teams probably talking to him pretty quickly."

As the front offices were talking, Coach Mazzulla had a sense of calm. He'd first met Holiday in the 2023 NBA

All-Star Game. Both player and coach are very religious and learned that they used the same Christian app. "I always had this spiritual hunch that our paths were going to connect somehow," Mazzulla said. "I didn't know if it was going to be spiritual, I didn't know if it was going to be a charity, I didn't know if it was going to be coaching. So when he got traded to the Blazers, I knew he was coming here."

You look back at how seamlessly Holiday fit in, and it's hard to believe that Stevens wasn't sure about making the move. "Even though I knew it was the right move, it was still hard to make that decision because there is risk associated with moving on from guys that have good corporate knowledge of the situation, are really good people and players," he said. "I felt really good about our team heading into the year. I felt better once Jrue got here."

The trade was going to hurt. Giving up two first-round picks, Malcolm Brogdon, and defensive stalwart Rob Williams is a lot. But with Porzingis in tow, I think they figured the middle was fine, and Holiday was a Celtic. Losing Williams wasn't easy. He'd developed into a terrific player who fit in with the stars on the team, but as I mentioned, that was only when he was available.

Brogdon was only in Boston for a year, but he won the NBA's Sixth Man Award.

He had also won Rookie of the Year when he played for Milwaukee, then played three nondescript years for the Indiana Pacers. Much like Williams, Brogdon wasn't lacking in ability, but *avail*ability—the 67 games he played in Boston were the most in a single season since his first year. I didn't talk to Brogdon much, but the other knock on him was that maybe he was just too smart. In speaking with some Pacers folks, they said he just took too much control in the locker room. Obviously on this team, you have the Jays. So you have to kind of relinquish the keys to the car. They are like the designated drivers, but it seems like Brogdon wanted to drive, as if he didn't trust them behind the wheel.

Holiday coming to Boston had to be a shock around the league. "You got to have three stars in the league, right?" Dan Shaughnessy of *The Boston Globe* said. "But I didn't know what a great defender he was, what a great adult he was, all those things, and the corner three that he could bring to it. There was a lot to like there. It was evident right from the jump. And, yeah, so that was an embarrassment of riches when they added him onto it."

Stevens was prescient about who Holiday was and how he'd fit in on this team. "He's a very coachable great teammate, wants to help others. That's just in his nature. That's who he is," Stevens said. "So all of his experiences, I think, will be like appropriately shared to help, right? And I think that there's a balance leadership-wise in that."

Days before he got traded, Holiday told the *Milwaukee Journal-Sentinel* where his head was at. "Before I even won here, I think I said, 'I'm a Buck for life.' And I mean that like deep in my heart. I don't want to play for any other team. I think we have a chance to continue to do great things as the Bucks team and organization, so I want to be in Milwaukee."

But he not only got traded, but also found out about it mere minutes before everyone else in the world did. "I felt like I—not that I was untouchable—but maybe I had done enough to at least let me know 24 hours in advance, not five minutes in advance. And maybe I'm asking for too much. I don't know," he said. "But it's kind of like, we won. I won there. You know what I'm saying? We won there. So, how many championships in Bucks history?"

But Holiday deserves a lot of credit. He could have blasted the Bucks, but he took the high road. "I still love the guys on the team, you know what I'm saying? But I also want to beat them," he explained. "It's not like in spite. I didn't go there in spite of them. I went there because that's my best chance of winning. And again, it ended up working out to where I feel like the Celtics equally wanted me, too…I wasn't going there like, 'Yeah, I'm gonna get back at the Bucks.' It was like, 'Well, I'm gonna go there and win.'"

That doesn't mean the transition for a West Coast guy who played at UCLA was easy. "Growing up a Lakers fan, that was probably the weirdest part for me," he said. "Like being in that green, being a Celtic, knowing that I was gonna sign to be a Celtic was like, like, am I betraying my roots, like where I came from?"

Holiday quickly learned the expectations here are, well, intense. "Being in that Celtic green, bro, like the pressure, it's different," he observed. "All they talk about here is winning. And the only thing that is important is winning."

CHAPTER TEN

THE NEW-LOOK CELTICS

For most teams, going to Game Seven of the Conference Finals would be a successful season. But, of course, the Boston Celtics have never been like most teams. Sure, they fought back from a 3–0 deficit against the Miami Heat and probably would have won if Jayson Tatum hadn't sprained his ankle. But he did, they didn't, and Brad Stevens made some pretty drastic moves. Right after the playoffs, he traded for Kristaps Porzingis and watched Grant Williams chase his free-agent fortunes with the Dallas Mavericks, signing a four-year deal worth more than $53 million. (Technically it was a sign-and-trade deal, but that was a formality.) Then, literally two days before the start of training camp, Stevens made the huge trade to get Jrue Holiday.

The team was loaded, but Stevens warned that things might start a little slowly—especially in regards to the massive expectations. "It's one thing that they've dealt with for a long time. So, I think we have really good people in that locker room. I don't think there's going to be anything but the desire to do well together," he told NBC Sports Boston. "I don't think we're a perfect team yet. I think we'll have to grow and build, and we'll see. We'll probably have our struggles early. And I don't think this team will freak out when it's not going well. I think this team will stay the course and continuously get better. And then hopefully we play our best at the end of the season, which we didn't do last year. And so, we'll see how it all plays out. It's a long year, and it's October."

So much for a slow start. The team won its first five games and 12 out of 15 to start the year. But there were still questions—specifically about the coach. Joe Mazzulla was dealt an impossible hand the previous year, taking over days before camp when Ime Udoka got suspended, then fired. And overall he did a great job, earning the permanent job by February.

But like all coaches, Mazzulla had his quirks; the first was his reluctance to call timeouts (preferring to let his team play through rough spots). Bob Ryan has covered every Celtics coach since Red Auerbach. Even *he* was puzzled by some of Mazzulla's lack of timeouts. "We know there are coaches that believe that you don't overreact and panic at certain times when things aren't going well, and you want them to play their way out of it kind of thing," Ryan said. "And on occasion I understand that. But he stubbornly went against all the norms in the beginning about when to call a timeout and when it was obvious that timeout was needed just to, 'Let's talk this over, guys. Let's stop this momentum here.'"

Personally, I understood this: Mazzulla grew on his team, and his team grew on Mazzulla. They believed in him. That first year he was trying to implement a system of the previous coach, Udoka. Eventually he needed to wipe that slate clean and make it *his* team. That's what happened in 2023–24.

With Holiday and Porzingis on board, I thought we had a chance to be good—like *really* good. Before the season tipped off, most people figured it would be Boston and the Milwaukee Bucks battling it out for Eastern Conference supremacy. The

Bucks obviously lost Holiday but added Damian Lillard. I didn't fear anyone, but certainly was concerned about what they could do...until I saw them, that is. Without Holiday leading the defense, this was not a team that had put fear in everyone's hearts.

The Cleveland Cavaliers figured to be tough. I'm a huge Donovan "Spida" Mitchell fan, and with Jarrett Allen and Evan Mobley, they had two bigs who could theoretically cause the Celtics problems. Probably the other team I was at least leery of was—believe it or not—the Orlando Magic. Their two best young players, Paolo Banchero and Franz Wagner, were only getting better and better. Banchero, specifically, is really good and has a huge ceiling as a player.

The calling card for this Celtics squad was going to be defense, and there has never been a backcourt in team history that guarded like Holiday and Derrick White. Anyone who knows me is aware of how much I loved my teammate Dennis Johnson, but who complemented him on the defensive end? Same thing for my favorite Celtics player in recent history, Marcus Smart. As great as he was, who paired up with him? Add these two guys, Holiday and White, together to the Jays, and then we're like the prison wardens, man. They come in here. The prison is locked down. I always say the initial point of attack is so important when you play the game.

Meanwhile, Mazzulla continued to grow in the job. He's a no-nonsense guy. His mentality is: I don't give a damn about being popular with the media. He's the Black Bill Belichick. He don't give a damn.

A great example happened in January. The Celtics pulled out an overtime win in Minnesota on a Wednesday night. The Jays, White, and Holiday all played about 40 minutes against the Timberwolves. And the 37-year-old Al Horford? He went 38 minutes because Porzingis was unavailable. The next night the Celtics had the early TNT game against the Bucks. So how did Mazzulla deal with this big Eastern Conference showdown? Well, as has been the case the past two seasons, Horford didn't play because it was a back-to-back contest. Porzingis came back and actually led the starters in minutes—with 21! You can probably guess how the game turned out.

We were down by 37 at halftime. For most of the third quarter, the deficit hovered around 40 points. A good fourth quarter of garbage time gave us a final of 135–102, and I'm telling you: it wasn't nearly that close. The point is that Mazzulla realized he had back-to-back games against two very good teams. There was no way they'd win both. So the guys sold out in the first one, rested in the second. Milwaukee was happy to beat the best team in the league, but Mazzulla was playing the long game. We call that a "schedule loss."

The other big question about Mazzulla from year one was his (over?)reliance on the three-pointer. In the Eastern Conference Finals loss to Miami, the Celtics put up an incredible 267 three-pointers but shot only 30 percent. (Not to be the old man, but to give you perspective, when we won the title in 1984, we took a *total* of 229! And made only 24 percent—and that was *with* a guy named Larry Joe Bird!) As a side note, I contributed one make in six attempts, LOL.

So although the team was stacked, there *were* still concerns both with the head coach and how to incorporate two huge new pieces.

* * *

After a drama-free regular season, it was time to play the games that really mattered. Winning 64 games was all good, but if the Boston Celtics came up short in the playoffs, that's all anyone would remember. There would be more calls to trade one of the Jays, and Joe Mazzulla's critics would have a field day. The heat was clearly on, and our first test would be against the Heat.

The last time we saw Miami, that familiar foe bolted out to a 3–0 series lead, then destroyed us in Game Seven. And, of course, they waited for us in Round One. This Miami team was shorthanded, as Jimmy Butler suffered a MCL injury in the play-in game win against the Philadelphia 76ers. The Celtics wouldn't have to deal with Playoff Jimmy this year. With or without Butler, there's no question in my mind that we'd win the series. The Heat had won 18 fewer games than us, but you know they always played better than their record.

The first game was a blowout as expected. Jayson Tatum had his first playoff triple-double en route to an easy 114–94 win. All was great in Celtic Land, but we've already known how good the team was as frontrunners. The next game would be a litmus test.

The whole knock against Miami was that it didn't have enough shooters. Maybe it was the three days between games, but good Lord, the Heat sure had enough on this night. Tyler Herro hit six three-pointers, and Caleb Martin made five of his six attempts. Miami shot 53 percent from downtown—21 percent better than Game One—and the Heat rolled to a 111–101 win. Some nights your opponent is just going to go nuts; that's the NBA, but you could feel the tension from the fanbase. We'd seen this movie before like when we led the Golden State Warriors 2–1 in the Finals—only to never win another game.

I still didn't think Miami had enough to beat us, but let's just say it would be a good idea to win Game Three. Kristaps Porzingis knew what was at stake. "We cannot take it for granted and be like 'Okay, we're going to be able to walk past them,'" he said. "So just maintaining that healthy edge for us is going to be very important."

K.P. wasn't the only Celtic who played terribly in Game Two, but he might have been the most noticeable, making only one of his nine shots, finishing with six points, and a -32. The Big Latvian wasn't going to let that happen again. "Just the way it burns inside after a game like that, a loss like that, I mean, probably having my worst game as a Celtic, it really burned inside, I'm not going to lie," he said. "I made some adjustments and didn't fall too much into their game of physical all the time. And that's what they want me to do. So, a completely different game today."

Yes, it was. A 42-point second quarter put this one away early. K.P. made amends for Game Two with 18 points, and things were back on track. We won 104–84.

Remember that quote from Porzingis about maintaining a "healthy edge?" *Healthy* was the key word and almost in a disastrous way. It happened with less than three minutes left in the first half. The Celtics were up by 16 on their way to an easy win and a commanding 3–1 series lead. KP and Jaylen Brown were running a pick-and-roll, as they'd done all season. Only this time Porzingis pulled up and immediately signaled to the bench. He was limping badly on his right leg. It didn't look good.

From the time he came into the league, nobody questioned Porzingis' ability, just his *avail*ability. He blew out his knee in year three and missed the entire next season. The year before he came to Boston was one of his healthiest, playing 65 games before the Washington Wizards sat him down to ensure a better draft pick. Even in this magical season with the Celtics, K.P. only played in 57 games. Granted, Joe Mazzulla handled him with kid gloves, and he sat out a few even when he was healthy, but this was the big fear: that he'd go down at the most inopportune time. It was like the damn haters had put this out there, and now it was reality.

I knew his being out was certainly a significant blow but also thought that the team had enough to beat any of the teams still playing. The Celts went on to win the game, but the only thing on everyone's minds was the health of K.P. "I hope that he can recover as fast as possible in the safest manner," Tatum said. "And I just hope that he's okay."

Derrick White's career high of 38 points was overshadowed by the Porzingis injury. "You hate to see that happen. He works so hard, one of the best players in this game,"

White said. "So I told him we got his back, and he's gonna do what he needs to do to get treatment and to do what he needs to do to get back with us."

Brad Stevens wasn't panicked, pointing out the team had been 22–4 without their big man. "Al Horford is proven and can morph himself into a four or a five, whatever you need, and I think that Luke and Xavier Tillman are two of the more underrated bigs in the league," he said. "So I actually felt pretty good about us getting through a round or a round and a half, but…there was a little bit of unknown if he was going to play at all."

As usual, Mazzulla was being…Mazzulla. "Nothing changes. Bringing the same mindset, intentionality, toughness, details to the next game regardless of who is available. It doesn't matter," he said. "All year we've had guys step in and play. So the most important thing is executing the gameplan and bring the mind-set and toughness it takes."

The series came back to Boston for Game Five. In previous years the team might have taken its foot off the gas and given Miami life. That wasn't going to happen this time around. White and Brown both went for 25 points, and the undermanned Heat were never in it. The guys did exactly what great teams do: blowing this one open, winning 118–84, wrapping up the series in five games. Tatum recapped it perfectly. "We should be learning from our mistakes and learning from things that we could have done better and applying it to next season, which we are doing this year," he said, "because we are trying to have a different outcome than we've had in the past."

CHAPTER ELEVEN

2024 EASTERN CONFERENCE SEMIFINALS

In round two we were waiting for the end of the Orlando Magic–Cleveland Cavaliers series. Then after Cleveland survived a wild seven-game series, we had our opponent. The Cavs have a good young team. They have a terrific 1-2 punch in the front court with bigs Jarrett Allen and Evan Mobley. Their two dynamic guards, Donovan Mitchell and Darius Garland, have been All-Stars.

Over the years I've gotten to know Mitchell a little bit. As it turns out, his dad played baseball at my alma mater, UNC-Charlotte. He was after my time—we didn't even have a baseball program when I was in school—but we usually get a chance to chat when our teams square off, saying things like, "Hey, is your dad here tonight?" I never had a doubt we'd beat the Cavs, but Mitchell is a beast. "Spida" can go ape—I mean, he scored 71 in one game—so we just needed to prevent a repeat. A lot of people don't think Spida and Garland can coexist, but I disagree. Mitchell doesn't need the ball to be effective, so he can play off of it. Garland does need it; so, the two of them work well together. The problem for them is that at 6'1" Garland isn't a great defender, and teams will always attack him. Spida is bigger, stronger, and faster, but Garland is their weak spot on D.

We all knew that Kristaps Porzingis wouldn't be playing in this series—the best hope was for him to be available in the Eastern Conference Finals—and that was certainly not a guarantee.

Cleveland had its own big injury—Allen suffered a rib contusion in the Orlando series and was day to day. Don't get me wrong: they weren't beating the Celtics either way, but I do think Allen would have made things tougher, especially given how Mobley played in the last couple of games when Mitchell was hurt. That's a strong duo.

This didn't figure to be much of a series, and Game One wasn't close. Mitchell had a huge performance with 33 points, six rebounds, and five assists. That was impressive, but Jaylen Brown was relentless, putting up 32 points, making four of his six three-pointers. Derrick White continued his ridiculous play with 25 points, and we won Game One by 25 points.

After the game D-White and J.B. exchanged verbal bouquets. "He's unbelievable," White said of Brown. "The things he can do on the court are special. I just think he consistently wants to get better, and he had it going, but he was also making the right read for myself and my teammates. And then when he has it going, it's fun to watch."

White certainly has had his moments in his two-and-a-half years in Boston, but he had become a certifiable weapon. "Derrick White has grown," Brown said. "This is a new version we haven't seen before. He's put the work in, his body has developed a little bit, he's got some more playoff experience, and he's being aggressive."

* * *

It's funny, but all the "experts" can't wait to label something a trend. The Cleveland Cavaliers came out firing in Game Two of this series, and Donovan Mitchell led the way. Spida did *everything*, finishing with 29 points, eight assists, and seven rebounds. The game was tied at halftime, but the Cavs blew it open from there en route to a 118–94 rout. "In the second half, it was scoring," Mitchell said. "Sometimes it's assists. Sometimes it's rebounds. Whatever it takes. And when it was time to go, it's time to go. I knew at some point I was going to have to start, obviously, shooting."

Shooting was the problem for the Boston Celtics. We shot 41 percent from the floor and 23 percent from three. "When we defend the way we defended and our shots fall, what we do travels," Cavs coach J.B. Bickerstaff said. "And we can win anywhere."

Okay, Coach. It was one game, and our guys couldn't hit the side of a barn. Let's not get carried away. Jayson Tatum played well with a 25-6-7 line, but the rest of the team struggled.

Because the Celtics lost Game Two against the Miami Heat, the headlines were now: "Why does Boston *always* struggle in Game Twos?" The loss dropped our home record to 15–14 during the past couple of years in the playoffs. So the other big narrative was: "Why can't the Celtics win at home?"

I still had no doubt about the series, and more importantly neither did Tatum. "The world thinks we're never supposed to lose. We're supposed to win every game by 25," he said. "And it's just not going to be like that all the time. So we don't expect it to be easy. It's a good team we're playing in the second round of the playoffs. It's going to be fun the rest of this series, especially come Saturday."

Fun would be the perfect word to describe Game Three in Cleveland. After a decent first half, the guys started the third quarter with 14 straight points to open up a 23-point lead that pretty much iced the game. Although we'd lost twice at the Boston Garden during the playoffs, we were straight-out warriors on the road, making it three straight away from home. Earlier in the season, the Cavs came back from 22 down to stun the Celtics in a big upset. That wasn't happening on this night.

Jrue Holiday scored 15 points in the first half to ensure that. "We felt like trying to punch them in the face right away was the right option," he said. "J.B. told us it wasn't over, and we knew that. We've been up 20 in the fourth quarter here, and they came back and won."

I loved the focus this team continued to show on the road. "We don't come to Cleveland for the weather. So, let's go," said Jaylen Brown, who went 13-of-17 from the floor. "There's nothing complicated about it: play defense, and the rest will take care of itself. We could have done better, but we kept them under 100."

And the D was great. Mitchell scored 33 points, but the rest of the Cavs combined for 60. To put this into focus, the Jays combined for 61 by themselves. The message was clear. The Celtics were the much better team, and they weren't messing around. "There was a purpose behind every play," Tatum said. "We did a good job communicating our actions."

One bit of noise that had started to percolate was the criticism of Tatum for not scoring at his normal rate. At this point in the playoffs, he was "only" averaging 23 points a night, down about five from his regular season. Well, in Game Four, he came out with 16 points in the first quarter and had 23 by halftime.

Sometimes people get on J.T. because of his laid-back nature, which reminds me of a guy who used to wear No. 31 for the Green back in the 1980s, but Tatum really did a great job of putting things into perspective. "I don't always agree with what [the critics] say. Maybe I feel like they're not watching everything else that I'm doing, but that's not my job to focus on that or give it any attention," Tatum said. "My job is to be the best player I can be for our team on any given night."

This wouldn't be the last time in the playoffs that Tatum had to answer criticism.

I knew this series was over, especially after we found out that Mitchell was out for Game Four with a calf strain. The Cavs gave it their all, but without Spida and Jarrett Allen, this wasn't a fair fight. Darius Garland went off for 30, but we won 109–102, a score that made the game seem closer than it really was. LeBron James sat courtside for this one, and Cleveland certainly could have used him.

One thing I loved about this team was the balance. Of course, the Jays were going to get their points (and they combined for 60 in this one), but the other guys almost took turns offensively. Some games it might have been Derrick White who scored a bunch, and other times it could have been Holiday, Kristaps Porzingis, or—on rare occasions—Al Horford.

Holiday has proven what he can do at that end of the floor. He'd averaged 19 points per game the previous year with the Milwaukee Bucks, but on a star-studded team like this, he would pick and choose when to step up. At this point in the playoffs, I observed that Holiday was starting to figure out his role in the offense. He had it going in Game Four and finished with 16 points on 11 shots. That meant White was going to take a little bit of a back season at that end of the floor, as he only took six shots but chipped in with seven boards and three assists. I wasn't the only one noticing what Holiday was doing. "He's starting to be more aggressive on the offensive," Joe Mazzulla noted. "When he's aggressive, both him, Derrick, and our bench, we're a different team."

With a 3–1 series lead, we came home for Game Five, and the guys weren't messing around. In Game Five White stepped up with 18 points, including 12 from distance, threw in five boards, six assists, and topped it off with two blocks.

And you know how we were just talking about how sometimes even Ol' Al can still take over a game? He was just dominant, going for 22 points, 15 boards, and five assists, joining James and Kareem Abdul-Jabbar as the only 37-year-olds to put up those types of playoff numbers. Spida Mitchell missed another game, and the undermanned Cavs had no shot, losing by 15. It would have been a total blowout if not for Evan Mobley, who scored a third of their 98 points with a dominating 33 inside.

It was pretty close midway through the second quarter with Cleveland actually leading 46–40. But an 18–6 Boston run put this out of reach. Mazzulla said the way the Cavs came out woke his team up. "It made us answer the bell," he said. "Guard your yard. The guys did it. It's a credit to them."

It was back to the Conference Finals for the third straight season. This was getting to be old hat—as it would be Brown's sixth time and Tatum's fifth. But would they be able to get over the hump?

CHAPTER TWELVE

A COMPETITIVE SWEEP

With the Cleveland Cavaliers out of the way, everyone was waiting to see who'd prevail in the Indiana Pacers–New York Knicks series. Everyone figured the Knicks would win, but they had huge injury problems, as Julius Randle was already out for the season, and midseason pickup OG Anunoby went down in Game Two with a hamstring injury. He tried to come back in Game Seven, but his return was short-lived.

Even though the Knicks were shorthanded, it was an entertaining series, as Jalen Brunson carried the Knicks to Game Seven, averaging nearly 30 a game and surpassing 40 twice. But Indiana had its own move that paid off in a huge way, getting Pascal Siakam, Anunoby's teammate from the Toronto Raptors. The two-time All-Star and NBA champion was a great fit with Myles Turner in the front court. At guard the Pacers had one of the true stars in the league—Tyrese Haliburton—and also Andrew Nembhard, who we'd learn is a huge pain in the butt.

They also had a familiar face: Aaron Nesmith. Billed as a sharpshooting assassin when the Boston Celtics drafted him out of Vanderbilt, things never worked out for him here. We used to call him "Crash" because he was always flying around 100 mph with no damn brakes. I don't know if I'd say he has totally made himself into a different player, but the game has definitely slowed down for him. Sometimes that takes a year, sometimes two, or sometimes it never comes. Nesmith has learned that he can be in gears two or three; he doesn't always have to be in fifth. And when he was in Boston, he'd always be leaning on his shot; his feet were never set. Now it's like they're in cement.

In addition to Nesmith, the Pacers had strong veterans like perpetual pest T.J. McConnell. Plus, there was also a championship coach and former Celtics players in Rick Carlisle. Indiana escaped a Game Seven in New York, but that didn't stop Knicks Nation from yapping. New York fans just crack me up. They had a nice team with all the Villanova guys like Brunson, Donte DiVincenzo, and Josh Hart. But I'm here to tell you that if they'd advanced, they would have gotten *smoked*. And truth be told, I think even Knicks fans know this deep in their hearts. A guy came up to me during the 2023–24 season and said how much he wanted his Knicks to dance with Boston. I asked him how he thought it would work, and *he* even said they'd get smoked, but he thought it would be fun to have a huge series in Madison Square Garden.

My broadcast partner, Sean Grande—a New York native—was convinced they'd be the Celtics' opponent in the Eastern Conference Finals, but everyone was wrong. The Pacers were young and hungry and didn't know any better.

The Eastern Conference Finals weren't supposed to be close, but someone forgot to tell Indy. We all knew the Celtics were the better team; that wasn't an issue. But if there was one thing I was a little concerned about, it was Game One.

Would we have a letdown that the Pacers were here—not the Knicks, which would have been the sexy matchup that everyone wanted?

My fear was realized, as Game One was an old-fashioned shootout. Turner, Haliburton, and Siakam all scored more than 20 points, as did Jayson Tatum, Jaylen Brown, and Jrue Holiday. Joe Mazzulla mentioned that Holiday was getting more comfortable in the offense, and he was right on. Game One was the first time he'd dropped 20 in a game since February. "Jrue came out and balled, man," Brown said. "He's the reason why we won this game."

This thing went back and forth; it was like a football game where whoever has the ball last wins. Indiana just would not miss, shooting 53 percent against the best defense in the league.

"Some of those guys turned into fucking Michael Jordan or whatever," Brown said. "In the fourth quarter, we made some big-time plays. Jayson Tatum made some big-time plays...We just had a great, great, grit win tonight." It was a chaotic game to say the least. "That's a great word," said Tatum, "because that shit was chaos. That shit was wild."

The Pacers' youth and inexperience showed, as they blew a three-point lead in the closing minute while committing two huge turnovers. You can't give a team like the Celtics any chance to breathe because here's what happens. With six seconds left, Brown hit an incredible double-pump fall-away three to send the game to overtime. This shot will live on in Boston sports history. It was that big. Clearly, J.B. wasn't intimidated by the stage. "Man, that was a tough shot," Al Horford said, "a very tough shot."

In the pantheon of huge Celtics shots, that one is right there. Brown looked like he was in a phone booth surrounded by the enemy. He had Pacers in front of him, on both sides, and Carlisle and the bench behind him. The only other shot I've seen that could compare is Larry Bird making a steal, dribbling up the court, and banking a jumper in Game Seven vs. Dr. J and the Philadelphia Sixers in 1981 to clinch our comeback from a 3–1 deficit.

I guess you can also throw in Dennis Johnson's three-pointer in Game Four of the 1985 Finals against the Los Angeles Lakers—the one after Bird said we needed a heart transplant and played like a bunch of "sissies." Bird's got us to the Finals, D.J.'s was *in* the Finals, and Brown's was in Game One of the Eastern Conference Finals. "It's simple: big-time players make big-time plays," Tatum said. "That was a hell of a shot."

In the extra five minutes, it became Tatum Time. J.T. looked like a man possessed, scoring 10 points, including a dagger three to give the Celtics a lead they wouldn't relinquish.

Indiana provided a wake-up call, and the Celtics answered it. "We didn't necessarily play well enough where we may have deserved to win," Tatum said. "J.B. gave us a second chance by hitting that shot, and we just talked about it in the huddle. 'We've got a second chance. Let's take advantage of it.'"

The Pacers were left to mourn a chance to steal the game. Coach Carlisle blamed himself. "This loss is totally on me," he said. "With 10 seconds in regulation, we should've just taken the timeout, advanced the ball, found a way to get in, made a free throw or two, and ended the game, but it didn't happen, and we made some other mistakes, but our guys just need to concentrate on fighting the way they fought in this game from start to finish, and we'll be back Thursday."

Carlisle is one of my favorite coaches, but this was a brain fart—plain and simple. In my mind this was a critical game. Yes, I knew how much better we were than Indiana, but pulling this out gave the guys the self-confidence to move forward. There were so many things that had to go right for this to happen. The Celtics should have lost, and if they did, maybe the series is a dogfight. Given what the media and fans would have said, who knows? Maybe the Celtics never would have recovered.

To me this was a dagger for the Pacers. A young team gets one opportunity to win on the road, and Brown crushed them with the three. Indiana probably wasn't winning this series anyway, but it definitely wasn't after that.

* * *

Game Two came on the heels of Jaylen Brown learning that he hadn't been selected to the All-NBA team. Combine that with how he rescued the team in the first game, and I had a feeling this would be J.B.'s night.

The Indiana Pacers actually led by two after the first quarter. That's when Brown went off. He had 17 points in the second quarter, taking it to the hole, hitting a three-pointer, and doing just about everything. There was no question Brown was focused, and perhaps that snub played a role in things. Though some players sulk about perceived slights, Joe Mazzulla pointed out that Brown uses it as fuel. "He cares about it in a way that motivates him, and I think he doesn't really care about it at all. He understands that winning is the most important thing," Mazzulla said. "He just cares about the right stuff."

For his part Brown stayed laser-focused on the task at hand. When asked about whether the snub motivated him, he was pretty succinct. "I wouldn't say that," he said. "I mean we're two games from the Finals. "So, honestly, I don't got the time to give a fuck."

I agree that he didn't need any more fuel to win a title. I remember how he looked after that loss in Game Seven against the Miami Heat the previous year. If there was a motivating factor for Brown, *that* was it.

After blowing the first game and then falling behind 2–0, Indiana got even more bad news when its superstar point guard Tyrese Haliburton went down with a hamstring injury. This was the same problem that cost him 10 games during the season. With him Indiana didn't have much of a chance. Without him that would be a big fat zero. But in the postgame news conference, everyone was talking about J.B.'s incredible 40-point performance, including his coach. "Jaylen is one of my favorite people," Mazzulla said. "He understands that winning is the most important thing."

Maybe the Celtics thought Game Three would be easy pickings without Haliburton. They were wrong. With the home crowd behind them, the Pacers came out on fire. No Haliburton, no problem. Andrew Nembhard, a second-year guard out of Gonzaga, was a pretty good player during the season, but knowing his team needed him, he played the half of his life, scoring 21 points in the first 24 minutes, including 3-of-3 from downtown, and the Pacers shot an incredible 64 percent from the floor. Jayson Tatum had 20, and Brown had 14, but the Celtics were down by 12 at the break. With just more than six minutes left in the third, the lead was 18. If the team expected a soft touch from their coach, they had another thing coming. "It was one of those timeouts in the third quarter," Tatum said. "Joe just told us to stop feeling sorry for ourselves."

I've been in this situation, and it's an emotional roller coaster. While the other team is going off, you have to try and stay poised, stay focused, and wait for the particular time where they're going to give you an opportunity to get back in that game. These Celtics were very patient. That is the Jrue Holiday factor. He's the guy you want on your side because he's so in control. You never see him too far up, never see him too far down. That's a huge difference. You all know how much I love Marcus Smart, but he'd be all jacked up, and then he'd be down. A lot of times you feed off what you see from your leader.

And by then we all knew that Mazzulla was a different breed. "Once we embraced the fact that we were down double digits on the road," Mazzulla said, "I thought it was pretty fun. I loved just the approach we took. I loved the mind-set we had...You have to be able to get through certain stuff, and I thought our guys did a great job of getting through it."

The players clearly bought in. "He really coached us. It was incredible just to see him going through so many progressions and so many things," Al Horford said. "And he's demanding of us, and it's something that we accept, and we're behind him, and we're trusting him, and that's what it took tonight."

By the fourth quarter, the Celtics' defense was back to normal. Indiana shot a measly 38 percent. Holiday hit all of his shots for nine points, and Tatum erupted, finishing with 36 points, 10 boards, and eight assists. The Celtics had won 114–111 and needed one more win to get back to the Finals.

I go back to Game Four in our 1984 series against the Los Angeles Lakers again. We'd been embarrassed in Game Three, but eventually it just hit us—these dudes ain't no better than us; they're just human. We have to play harder. We're more physical and the bigger bullies. We backed them into the corner and got them playing our game.

The Celtics smelled blood. They had no interest in bringing this series back to Boston.

Back in the day, Bill Fitch's thing was to bash your opponent against the wall. And believe me: when you're down three games to nothing, it's easy to let go of the rope. I know from firsthand experience. In 1983 we were about to get swept by the Milwaukee Bucks. *I'm sorry: there's no scenario that the Celtics should get beaten by the Bucks.* We were a team in disarray, and we knew that Fitch was going to get fired. And I want to stress that it's not like Kevin McHale, Robert Parish, Larry Bird, and myself said, "We're gonna get this asshole out of here." But you're not going to tell me that our front line was going to get beat by Paul Mokeski! Until... we did. We got smoked in Game Four, Fitch got fired, and we started our summer.

The Pacers weren't going to let go of the rope with Carlisle as their head coach and in Game Four they gave it their best, but it just wasn't enough. Nembhard continued to play out of his mind with 24 points, but Brown took over in the fourth, scoring 10 points in the last 12 minutes.

One of the best qualities about this team is having amnesia. It's like Tiger Woods. If he hits it into the water, what is he going to do? That shot is gone. He needs to focus on the *next* one. That mentality came in handy for this game. With 45 seconds left, the game was tied at 102. Derrick White, who had made only one of his eight three-point attempts, showed again how he's a cold-blooded killer by drilling one from the corner, wrapping up a 15–4 run, and helping send our boys to the Finals.

But before we got there, we had some business to tend to. I had been designated to hand out the Eastern Conference Finals MVP trophy. A lot of people don't know this, but there's a whole rehearsal that goes on the day before. Someone plays the role of ownership, of Brad Stevens, of Mazzulla, and so on. You go through everything to make sure it goes smoothly. ESPN/ABC's Lisa Salters was the host who controlled everything. The plan was that I'd hand the championship trophy to Wyc Grousbeck, and then Salters would tell me who the MVP was, and I'd present that.

That *was* the plan.

Because it was a close game, I wasn't able to leave my broadcast position until the end and then I booked it down to the court. Next thing I know, we were live. Salters handed me the trophy, and I gave it to Grousbeck. So far, so good.

Grousbeck started talking, and Salters and I were looking at each other; I was waiting to find out who had been voted MVP. Once Grousbeck was done, Salters explained that, "The MVP trophy is named after Larry Bird. And since Bird wasn't here, we had his teammate [me]." I had to laugh to keep from crying. There was still one problem—she never told me who was getting the trophy! I looked down at her notepad and was pretty sure I saw Jaylen's name scribbled—but I didn't have my glasses. If I was wrong, this would be a Steve Harvey moment from the Miss Universe pageant. I tried to have a pregnant pause, hoping she'd let me know, but she never did. So, I said, "How about them damn Celtics!" Fortunately, I was right in guessing J.B. and said, "It is my honor to present the trophy to Jaylen." And then I got the hell out of there!

Salters later apologized to me, but it was all good. And Brown? Well, he was surprised. "I wasn't expecting it at all," he said. "I never win shit."

Some talking heads tried to make it seem like Tatum was jealous of Brown for winning the MVP award, but I don't buy it at all. The fact is, though, it was close, and I do think the right guy got the honor. Look at Brown's incredible three in Game One, and then he went out and dropped 40 the next game. Tatum brought it home with 26 points, 13 boards, and eight assists in the last game, but Brown was more consistent, and I think both guys were just happy to be heading back to the Finals. "This team has trusted me, especially in this playoffs and those moments to just be who I am," Brown said. "I felt like I've been able to just deliver just being patient and being poised. Those opportunities have presented themselves, and I've been able to take advantage of them. But I give all my credit to my teammates for the trust they had in me to have the ball in my hands and to be able to make those plays."

People ask if this series—specifically the huge three-pointer—was a coming-out party for Brown. Maybe it was for the masses, but if you were really following the team, you knew that J.B. had been doing it all year. And the rest of the guys? Well, Mazzulla put it best. "You get to know these guys as people and you start to see how much they really care about doing anything and everything, what it takes to win," he said. "You see how it impacts their families, their marriages, their wives, all the traveling, everything we do. So just to see them to be vulnerable and open and just the sense of joy, it's kind of why you do what you do."

CHAPTER THIRTEEN

PORZINGIS SHINES

While things had gone according to plan in the Eastern Conference, there were a couple of big upsets out West. In the semifinals the Dallas Mavericks knocked out the top seed, the Oklahoma City Thunder, in six games. This was surprising but not shocking, as OKC was very young and probably a year or two ahead of schedule in its rebuild. Don't get me wrong: they're really good now, but things are only going to get better.

The other matchup was of huge interest to the Celtics. The defending champion Denver Nuggets had two wins against the Boston Celtics during the season—one in Boston and one in Denver. Nikola Jokic won his third MVP award in four years, Jamal Murray had been a huge playoff performer, and they also had really nice players in Michael Porter Jr. and Aaron Gordon.

But as often happens with defending champions, Denver lost a couple of key pieces in Bruce Brown and Jeff Green. That upset the applecart in terms of depth.

The Nuggets were going against the upstart Minnesota Timberwolves, who were in the midst of their most successful season ever. Minnesota had twin towers in Karl-Anthony Towns and Rudy Gobert along with rising star Anthony Edwards in the backcourt. The Timberwolves led the Western Conference most of the season before settling in as the No. 3

seed. Most people figured that like with OKC, Minnesota was a little bit ahead of schedule, but that it would give Denver a good series.

Where our sweep of the Indiana Pacers featured four hotly contested games, the first six between the Nuggets and Timberwolves only had one decided by seven or fewer points. Denver led by 15 at half—no team in NBA history had ever blown that big a halftime lead in a Game Seven—and eventually 20. But Edwards caught fire, and the Timberwolves stunned the defending champs to advance to the Western Conference Finals. Not that the Celtics were worried, but Jayson Tatum said that when the Nuggets were eliminated, he knew that he was going to become a champion. "I felt like Denver was the only team that matched up best with us," he said. "I thought that we were going to play Denver in the Finals, and it was going to be a good one."

Minnesota vs. Dallas was a weird series to me because I felt like the Timberwolves had that team of destiny thing going on. My current broadcast partner and former Timberwolves announcer Sean Grande said there was some computer simulation that came out saying it would be a Boston–Minnesota Finals. When you watched the Timberwolves, you figured it would be a hell of a series. Everyone knew about KAT, Gobert, Edwards, but for me a guy like Jaden McDaniels would be a key. I thought their physicality, size, and toughness was going to be an issue for the Mavs. But…it wasn't meant to be. Dallas caught a break because I think Minnesota was spent from its emotional win, and to be honest, it pretty much peed the bed against the Mavs. Behind Luka Doncic and our "old friend" Kyrie Irving, the Mavs won the series in five games and were heading to Boston for Game One of the NBA Finals.

As we prepared for the Finals, there were storylines aplenty. Of course, the Celtics faithful were thrilled to welcome back Irving with open arms. Would this be the year the Celtics finally got over the hump? And was Doncic the second coming of Larry Bird?

Um, wait on that for a second. I need to chime in on that one. Listen: Doncic is a bad man. Great player, extremely skilled, but don't try telling me he's the next Larry Joe Bird. In fact, I thought it was extremely disrespectful that the world just took it as fact that Doncic was the best player in this series. Hello, Mr. Tatum and Mr. Brown.

But anyway in my opinion, I always thought the best comp for Bird was Dirk Nowitzki, not Doncic. Don't get me wrong. Doncic can do a lot of things that Bird did: scoring the ball, creative passing, things like that. But what Doncic doesn't have—and would be proven in this series—is his toughness. Bird was like the rust you have on your old car. However that rust got there, you didn't want to put your hand in there because you'll get cut. Doncic is a great player, and he *does* have some similarities, but he ain't Bird, that's for sure.

As far as Mr. Irving goes, well, I'd like to think that Irving has matured a bit. Getting married and having kids seems to have settled him down a bit. I thought coming into the series that he would have an opportunity to do some things, but he didn't instill fear in my heart. I figured the pressure would get to him because he hadn't played well in Boston since the time he stomped on the leprechaun's face after that playoff game.

The 2023–24 season season was a renaissance for Irving. Where folks such as Kristaps Porzingis weren't able to gel with Doncic, Irving found his place. Why? I say it was the last call for alcohol. In other words, he'd pretty much run out of chances. We know what happened in Boston. Then he went to the Brooklyn Nets with Kevin Durant, and the shit eventually hit the fan. He came to Dallas and he just hit his stride like this was his chance to put an imprint on a season. There was a certain peace about him; we heard less about the Earth being flat, and there wasn't as much burning sage in the building. No, a lot of the theatrics were gone, and he just started playing—and that's something he's always been able to do. I'll say it until I'm blue in the face, but Kyrie Irving is the most talented guard ever to wear a Celtics uniform. There's been nobody like him. But did I think he could pull off this upset? Ummm…no.

* * *

Coming into the NBA Finals, everyone was talking about how this would be a classic series; many national talking heads even picked the Dallas Mavericks to win. In my opinion, this was ABC: Anybody But the Celtics. I just didn't see that happening. The media wanted to make our team into the Buffalo Bills—always coming close but never winning the whole enchilada. After coming up short several times, it was an easy thought to have. But it wasn't true.

There's no question the Boston Celtics had the better team; they'd been the best in the NBA all season long. Sure, the Mavs had some talent, but what really pissed me off was the narrative that Luka Doncic was the best player in the series. This was just about unanimously accepted, and it wasn't true. Doncic *is* an outstanding offensive player—nobody would argue that—but being a great *player* means defense, rebounding, etc. But how can he be the best player when Jaylen Brown has taken on the assignment of guarding the opposition's top player? Jayson Tatum had been lights out defensively and developed into a great rebounder.

The other thing with Doncic is that he was like a magnet for opposing offenses. Hunting out people is well established in the NBA. Back in my day, you'd find a guy who just couldn't guard someone—like the Philadelphia 76ers' Marc Iavaroni—and we'd keep throwing it to whoever was matched up with him. Even in the Finals when the Cleveland Cavaliers dethroned the Golden State Warriors, if you watch the tape, you'll see that every time the Cavs had a chance, they'd go to whoever Steph Curry was guarding. That's exactly what the Celtics did to Doncic. Not only is he a sieve defensively, but you also can wear him down by making him work. Brown attacked him, and so did Tatum. They made sure to put his ass in the popcorn popper. I didn't care what anyone said; *those* were the two best players in this series.

Now truth be told, I *was* a little nervous because I thought the Celtics were the best team the previous season as well. And in the last couple of seasons, they hadn't played as well in big spots as you'd like. But then I looked at it and realized that this was a completely different team. These weren't the guys who lost to Golden State or the Miami Heat. Sure, many of the players were still there, but this team was stacked with more weapons, and they were a much tighter group.

In the cover story for *Time* magazine's 100 Most Influential Rising Stars issue, Brad Stevens recalled a conversation with Brown before the NBA Finals. Brown locked eyes with Stevens and said, "Big fucking two weeks."

"I was like, 'Oh man, we're going to be hard to beat,'" Stevens recalled. "He knew what was coming and he was ready to take advantage of it. Our whole team was like that. He spoke that confidence loudly. It was not arrogant. It was, 'This is what it takes. And we're going to do everything we can to do it.'"

But the huge question before Game One was whether Kristaps Porzingis would play or not. The secondary question was how effective he would be after missing 38 days with an injury.

I knew that K.P. was going to be out there. I'd seen him in the hallway a couple of days before and told him that the team needed him. He looked at me and just smiled and said, "I feel good. I feel strong right now, I'm ready to go."

But that doesn't mean he was convinced. He told ESPN, "It was getting longer than expected. You're like, *Am I going to be good? Am I going to be in shape for the final?* It's tough. I'm not going to lie. It's tough just to prepare for that mentally."

Joe Mazzulla was guardedly optimistic. "Obviously, you can't simulate the speed and intensity of the game, which I think just comes with a little bit of reps," he said. "K.P.'s a great player. Just because he's been out for a month doesn't mean you have to relearn how to play basketball. I expect him to pick right back up where he left off. Obviously, there will be a little bit of rust."

But nobody could have possibly envisioned what happened next.

Back in the 1970 Finals, the New York Knicks hosted the Los Angeles Lakers in a winner-take-all Game Seven. All-Star center Willis Reed had missed the previous game with a torn thigh muscle. The league's MVP was considered questionable at best for the showdown. Suddenly, the Madison Square Garden crowd started to stir, and ABC analyst Jack Twyman exclaimed, "I think we see Willis coming out!"

On the first two Knicks possessions, Reed then hit jumpers. He didn't score another point all game, but the damage was done—he'd given his team a boost that they would ride all the way to the title.

When K.P. came out for warmups, joining his teammates in wearing special Bill Walton T-shirts, which commemorated the passing of the Hall of Famer 11 days before, the Garden erupted. "Obviously, what helped me is just even from the walk out before the game and then getting on the court, getting that kind of support was unreal," Porzingis said. "The adrenaline was pumping through my veins."

You and me both, brother.

When he got off the bench, it somehow got even louder. Less than five minutes into the first quarter and with the Celtics leading 12–11, K.P. checked in. K.P. was fouled on his first shot by Doncic and made the two free throws. The next trip on offense, Jaden Hardy ended up trying to guard Porzingis. Let's so some quick math. K.P. is 7'2", and Hardy is 6'4". That's a *ten-inch* advantage. *How do you think that turned out?*

K.P. faked Hardy out, then knocked him on his ass, and drilled the jumper.

Two minutes later, K.P. picked on someone (almost) his own size, shaking 7'1" rookie Dereck Lively for a huge jam. He was moving like a damn gazelle. Right after that, he turned into 6'5" Josh Green, nailed him in the man parts, and hit another jumper. Oh, and for good measure, Payton Pritchard hit him trailing the fast break, and K.P. threw up a 30-footer. Nothing. But. Net. I was like, "Dude, you haven't played in more than a month, and *that's* the shot you want to take?"

In just more than seven minutes of action, he was like Willis Reed on steroids: 11 points (on 4-of-5 shooting), three boards, and two enormous blocks. This was one of the most incredible things I've seen on a basketball court. By the end of the quarter, the score was 37–20—the largest first-quarter lead since at least 1998. This was part of an incredible 44–14 run, and this thing was over—almost.

K.P. finished the night with 20 points, six boards, and three blocks—in only 21 minutes. He was blissfully unaware of what he was doing. "This kind of game, I was just in the moment," he told ESPN. "I didn't even catch that I had 18 at half. I was just hooping, and it's just happening naturally. Those are the best kind of games. You're just so in the moment and so locked in. You're just...the time just flies by."

There was no chance he wasn't going to take advantage of a moment he'd waited his whole life for. "It was tough," he said. "I was just doing my rehab, supporting the guys, being around the team as much as I could, stay engaged, and guys were taking care of business, and now I finally got my chance to be out there with them and I enjoyed that game like never before."

Nobody who was in the building could believe what we just saw, including Stevens. "[It was] otherworldly, maybe, maybe the best performance off of an injury I've ever seen," he said. "It was just incredible."

The only time I've heard the Boston Garden crowd this loud was in Game Six of the 2008 Finals, when Kevin Garnett, Ray Allen, and Paul Pierce just kicked the crap out of the Lakers.

Mazzulla was confident all along regarding K.P.'s comeback. "It doesn't matter how long he takes off," he said, "the guy is going to make plays because of how talented he is and the work he puts in."

Porzingis put his epic night into perspective. "I've had so many unfortunate situations, and then having to come back, it kind of prepared me," he said. "And then having to jump back in at the highest-level game, the biggest stage...I think all I've been through in my career prepared me for that moment and I proved it once again to myself and everyone else that I'm capable of doing that."

And give Coach Mazzulla credit. I thought they should have started Porzingis because a lot of times when you go through warmups and get loose, it's best to keep you out there instead of cooling off on the bench. But once again, Mazzulla knew what he was doing, and it resulted in a performance that wowed Al Horford. "His energy was unbelievable on offense, on defense, the chase-down block in transition," Horford said. "His energy just got us going and took us to another level."

Tatum stated the obvious. "We're a great team when guys are down, but we're really, really special when we have everybody," he said. "That was a big spark for us to start the game."

Having K.P. able to play was the X-factor that nobody would have an answer for. "He's a matchup nightmare," Derrick White said. "Even when you play good defense, he doesn't really see you. It's been unreal just watching him all year. Then defensively, he uses his size well, just impacts the games in so many different ways. He changes us, and he makes us a better team."

K.P.'s buddy, Jaylen Brown, was practically beaming. "It was amazing," he said. "Nobody's more proud or more excited for him than I am."

During the 44–14 run, I thought the Garden might actually explode when Brown shook Doncic, then absolutely posterized Kyrie Irving and Daniel Gafford. Brown has always been able to do the spectacular on offense, but it was his defense on Doncic that got his coach's attention. "What you saw tonight is kind of the challenge he took for himself coming into the year: not wanting to be defined by one thing," Mazzulla said, "wanting to make plays, wanting to be a well-rounded player and get better and better."

His partner in crime, Tatum, noticed as well. "J.B.'s somebody that has worked on his craft year after year," he said.

"It's special to see when guys put in the work and it translates on the court."

Give Dallas credit: it went on a 35–14 run to make it an eight-point game with less than five minutes left in the third. But the Celtics answered that and then some, closing out the quarter on a 14–2 run, going into the fourth quarter with a 20-point lead.

Brown was never worried. "That's the game. When a team goes on a run, you got to manage it, you got to stay composed, and you got to keep playing basketball," he explained. "It's almost like you just have short-term memory a little bit."

Mazzulla's gameplan was perfect: attack Doncic on defense. The so-called "best player" in the series wasn't in top shape and didn't seem particularly interested in working on that end of the floor. He finished with 30 points and 10 rebounds but was a -10 on the night.

But Porzingis' historic performance was the story of the night. "It was too good to be true, things you gotta be kidding me," sportswriter Bob Ryan said. "The other thing is I'm fond of saying, 'In a matter of truth versus fiction, truth plus the points every time.'"

I love myself some K.P. He may look and sound like Ivan Drago from *Rocky IV*, but he's funny as hell. "Tonight was an affirmation to myself that I'm pretty good, you know?" he said, "Maybe I'm not perfect, but I'm pretty good, and I can play like this and I can definitely add to this team."

Of course one of—if not the—biggest stories coming into the series was Irving's return to Boston. Although it did seem like Kyrie was more settled off the court, I didn't expect him to have a big series. He said he sprained his thumb after banging it on Tatum's arm, and maybe that did affect him in Game One. But there was more to it.

When Irving is playing well, you can feel the sense of calm in his game. Against OKC in the conference finals, he was seeing the game in slow motion, just like when he won a title with the Cleveland Cavaliers by hitting the huge shot to beat Golden State. That wasn't the case in Game One. It was clear that he had a lot of nervous energy. It was like he was on pins and needles, *thinking* about what to do instead of just *doing* it. It's obvious the vitriol from the fans had its desired effect. There was just a lot of angst with Irving. People always ask if I'd get nervous before a game, and, of course, I would. But once the ball went up in the air, those nerves were gone.

Irving never seemed to get past the fans' furor. It was like he was trying to keep all of that under wraps. There were clearly a lot of things going on in his head that shouldn't have been. He only made six of his 19 shots, missed all five from three, and ended up with a -19.

Some Boston Celtics fans were upset when the team drafted Jaylen Brown third overall in the 2016 NBA Draft, but it obviously turned out to be an excellent pick.

From left to right: Steve Pagliuca, Wyc Grousbeck, Jayson Tatum, Danny Ainge, and Brad Stevens meet the media, following the 2017 NBA Draft. While Markelle Fultz was the presumed pick, the Boston Celtics pulled off a draft heist by trading back and selecting Tatum.

Brooklyn Nets guard Kyrie Irving steps on the Boston Celtics' leprechaun logo after defeating the Celtics in the 2021 playoffs, but the Celtics would get the last laugh against Irving in the 2024 NBA Finals.

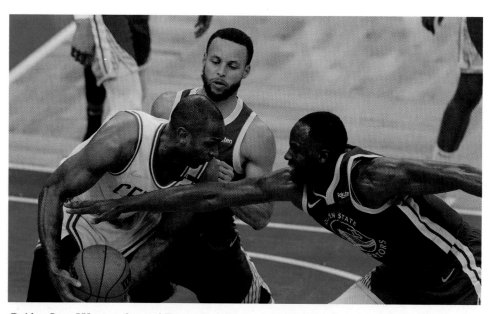

Golden State Warriors forward Draymond Green and guard Stephen Curry defend Al Horford as the Warriors close out the Boston Celtics in the 2022 NBA Finals.

Jayson Tatum, who suffered an injury in Game Seven, defends Jimmy Butler, who led all players with 28 points while guiding the Miami Heat to a Game Seven win on our home court to send the Heat to the 2023 NBA Finals.

Jayson Tatum and the Boston Celtics get revenge against the Miami Heat, defeating them 118–84 in Game Five of the 2024 NBA playoffs.

Jaylen Brown hits a game-tying three-pointer against the Indiana Pacers to send Game One of the 2024 Eastern Conference Finals into overtime.

Boston Celtics center Kristaps Porzingis celebrates after hitting a three-pointer as part of his spectacular injury comeback during Game One of the 2024 NBA Finals.

In addition to providing his usually terrific defense against Dallas Mavericks star Luka Doncic, Jrue Holiday also had 26 points and 11 rebounds in Game Two of the 2024 NBA Finals.

Derrick White, who was thorn in the Dallas Mavericks' side all series long, goes against former Boston Celtics guard Kyrie Irving in Game Two of the NBA Finals.

Dallas Mavericks head coach Jason Kidd tried to plant seeds of dissension, but the Jays show their love for each other after winning their first title together.

Jayson Tatum celebrates the 2024 NBA title with his son Deuce.

Jayson Tatum sprays champagne in his home locker room after defeating the Dallas Mavericks in Game Five of the NBA Finals.

As part of his 21-point performance in Game Five of the NBA Finals, Jaylen Brown throws down a tone-setting dunk in the first half.

NBA Finals MVP Jaylen Brown celebrates the championship win with his team.

CHAPTER FOURTEEN

KIDD'S MIND GAMES

The Boston Celtics executed the game plan to perfection in Game One. But the national narrative was still all in on the ABC (Anybody But the Celtics) bandwagon. Longtime NBA veteran (and three-time champion) Danny Green didn't think they could repeat their performance in Game Two. "It was a hell of a win for them, but Dallas found some things," he said on *The Draymond Green Show*. "I wouldn't be too confident after watching tonight's game. Ky didn't have a great game. And I don't think the energy, Porzingis is going to be able to sustain that…Luka, it took him a quarter to settle in, but once he settled in, he's found something. He knows where he's at, now Ky just has to settle in. Once that happens, we're gonna have a series. It's gonna be a real series."

To Mr. Green, I'd say, "How'd that work out?"

I'm not sure that Jason Kidd was feeling as confident. Knowing that the media was already trying to compare the Jays, J-Kidd tried to stir shit up, maybe to distract everyone from the simple fact that his team was outmatched. "Well, Jaylen's their best player," Kidd said. "Just looking at what he does defensively, he picked up Luka full court, got to the free-throw line, he did everything. That's what your best player does. He plays both sides, defense and offense, at a high rate. He's been doing that the whole playoffs. When you talk about the Eastern Conference MVP, it seems like he's continuing to pick up where he left off."

People ask me what I thought J-Kidd's motivation was. My answer is an easy one—he was doing anything he could to get in their heads. Now did it turn out that Brown was the best player in that series? Yes, but Jayson Tatum has been the leader of the team, the top scorer, and facilitator. I think Kidd saw the writing on the wall and thought he needed to do something to prevent the ship from sinking.

This is where the Celtics' maturity came into play. "J-Kidd, man, I see what he's doing. I see what he's doing," veteran Al Horford said, laughing.

Brown also refused to take the bait. "I have no reaction," he said. "I don't know. I think it's a team game. We're trying to focus on that, and everybody has their own opinions."

Almost on cue Tatum echoed his teammate's sentiments. "No reaction. This is a team sport. We understand that. We wouldn't be here if we didn't have J.B. on our team. We can say that for a lot of guys," he said. "We all played a part in getting to where we're at. We understand that people try to drive a wedge in between us. I guess it's a smart thing to do or to try to do. But we've been in this position for many years of guys trying to divide us and say one of us should be traded, or one is better than the other. So it's not our first time at the rodeo."

Bob Ryan, who's covered Kidd since he came into the league in 1994, had an interesting perspective as he usually does. "I really don't know enough about the way he thinks, but if in fact he did that as a ploy, I remember that's good gamesmanship. I mean, it's not foul. That's not cheating, that's not unfair play, fine. I don't know what he meant by it. Does he really believe it? I have to question that, that he can really believe it. But if he does, well, maybe he's not as good a talent evaluator as maybe he should be," Ryan said. "If he did it, then, well, he's more, a little more clever in that regard than I thought. I'm not kidding you. I think there's nothing wrong with that. He definitely had the inferior team...And so anything he tries is fair game because he's playing a team that is markedly better than his."

Another sign of desperation came from Irving. As expected the Boston crowd booed him every time he touched the ball in Game One. Never a shrinking violet, he tried to take the pressure off his teammates by saying he thought the crowd would be even louder. This was all about deflection, but it wasn't really a great idea. It was like getting bitten by a lion, then saying, "Oh, I thought he was going to eat a couple of more limbs." C'mon, man.

It's funny. My broadcast partner, Sean Grande, told me that by the end of the series, Irving would no longer be Public Enemy No. 1 and that Luka Doncic would be because he'd score so many points. Ummm, no.

Irving did play better in Game Two—but still made only seven of his 18 shots (none from three), and Doncic had a 32-11-11 triple double but also had eight turnovers, as the Celtics went up 2–0 with a 105–98 win. This game was a microcosm of what made this team so special. Tatum missed 16 of his 22 shots but had nine boards and 12 assists.

Brown picked up the slack with 21 points and seven assists of his own.

But the big story—just like Game One vs. the Indiana Pacers—was Jrue Holiday. He's so smart. He knows exactly when and where to pick his spots. And in this one, he went for a team-high 26 points, and the 6'4" guard added 11 rebounds. Kristaps Porzingis had a predictable letdown after his incredible return to action, but it didn't matter. As always, Joe Mazzulla had his players' backs. "I'm really tired of hearing about one guy or this guy or that guy, and everybody trying to make it out to be anything other than Celtic basketball," he said. "Everybody that stepped on that court today made winning plays on both ends of the floor."

Even Doncic had to give the Celts some props. "That's why they are the No. 1 team in the NBA with the No. 1 record," he said. "They have a lot of great players. Basically, anybody can get off."

Holiday is a guy who cares about one thing—winning. His last year in Milwaukee, he averaged 19 points a game. His first year in Boston? 12.5—the lowest scoring output since his rookie year. Do you know how many times he complained about his role? That would be zero.

Meanwhile, through the first two games of the NBA Finals, Holiday had 38 points, *19* rebounds, eight assists, and *no* turnovers. The last guy to do that to open up the Finals? Some guy named Michael Jordan in 1998. It was clear to me that the Mavs were trying to guard the Jays differently and basically saying, "Jrue, we're going to let you have the shots."

Well, Holiday took full advantage. That's what made this team so incredible all year—Boston always had the answer. In this game it was Holiday, and then Derrick White stepped up on offense and defense. It's like the Celtics had plan A, B, C, and D.

With just under a minute to go, the Celtics led by five when Tatum had a shot blocked, and Dallas stormed up the court. Irving made a nice pass to P.J. Washington, who went in for the finish…only to get stuffed by D-White. Game over and series (basically) over. The thing with White is he just comes up with these blocks that defy logic since he's only 6'4." He has incredible timing in a way he reminds me of the late Dikembe Mutombo. I remember Dennis Johnson would always pull up his left hand, talking about how he was blocking shots. White moves like that. He finished 16th in the entire NBA in blocked shots last year, and that was the best among guards. There are a lot of times when someone breaks in like Washington did, and you're thinking, *Just don't foul him!* Then White would come back and do it in such an efficient manner.

He and Holiday are probably the most stealth backcourt in the entire league. Holiday was asked about the Jays' off night and Kidd's comments about Brown being the better player.

"How they play together is sacred, and something that can't be broken," Holiday said. "I don't prefer one or the other. I prefer both because they're both superstars, and they're showing it on the biggest stage in the world."

And here's the simple fact: Doncic and Irving played really well...and Dallas still lost. I'd seen how they played on the road against Oklahoma City and Minnesota, and when that backcourt got rolling, that duo was tough to beat. The Celtics were different though. "At the end of the day, they are better than all the teams we've played," Washington said. "It's the Finals, and we've just got to be better...Their record says that they have been the best team all year. They have two superstars, they have a lot of great role players, and they play team ball. So, we've just got to be better."

* * *

Everyone felt pretty good after the first two games. The Boston Celtics held serve on their home court and were a couple of wins away from winning the title. The Jays were playing well, and the backcourt of Jrue Holiday and Derrick White stepped up as needed. Of course, much of the buzz was still surrounding what Kristaps Porzingis had done in the first game, an all-time playoff heroic effort.

In Game Two, though, Porzingis pulled up lame again. This time it was something in his left ankle. (His injury against the Miami Heat was his right side.) The Celtics still won the game, but this was a big deal. My initial reaction began with an F and ended with a K. Let's just say if you were sitting next to me, you could smell my fear. Plus, the injury happened on what was basically a non-contact play, which is never good.

For his part the big guy didn't seem overly concerned; in fact, he wanted to stay out there. "I'll die out there if we need. So, I just kept going," he said. "But obviously I was a little bit limited. So the smart thing was to get Al back in there and close out the game."

On the one hand, K.P. had to do his postgame interviews while sitting down, but he was very confident that he'd be ready for Game Three in Dallas. "I feel good. Obviously, something happened a little bit, but I have a couple days [to get ready] again, and believe me: we'll do everything we can to be back and moving."

Of course, athletes are usually the last ones to admit defeat. So, it wasn't a surprise when K.P. sounded optimistic. "That's something I'll leave in the medical staff's hands to determine whether I can go or no," he said. "But from my side, as I said, nothing is going to stop me unless I'm told I'm not allowed to play. That's the only reason I would not be out there."

But the team was using words like "rare" and "serious," which is never a good sign. It turned out K.P. had a torn medial retinaculum, with a tendon dislocation. Now I don't have a medical degree. So, I'll borrow from *The Boston Globe*, who interviewed Dr. Miho Tanaka, an orthopedic surgeon and the director of women's sports medicine for Mass General Brigham hospital for some clarification. She said it was like a bad ankle sprain with some added layers. Most sprains—as my coauthor, who is recovering from his 20th ankle surgery, can attest—happen when the ankle rolls outward. If the opposite happens, that's when you can get damage to the tendons that attach muscles to the bone. "There is a tendon [on the inside of the ankle] called the posterior tibialis tendon," Tanaka told *The Globe*, "which basically attaches the bone to the posterior tibialis, which is a muscle that helps to point your toes toward each other. That tendon runs under that bone that sticks out on the inner side of your ankle, the ones that touch when you bring your feet together. That bone serves as almost like a pulley for this tendon. And so what can happen is that if your foot goes into that extreme position, where the sole of your foot is facing outwards, then that the tendon, which is running as a pulley under the bone, can pop out of that area and over the bone."

All I know is that didn't sound good, and everyone was certainly nervous about if/when we'd see K.P. again.

CHAPTER FIFTEEN

TEXAS TWO-STEP

I t's one of the oldest adages in sports: "We've just got to get one on the road." The favored team wins the first two games at home, and all it needs to do is win one on the road and then come home to close it out. Sometimes it's easier said than done, though. The Boston Celtics were without Kristaps Porzingis, who had a rare tendon issue in his left ankle called a torn retinaculum and dislocated posterior tibialis tendon. I didn't know what all that meant—except that we probably wouldn't be seeing him again in the Finals.

With the best record in the NBA, it goes without saying that if the Celtics won all their home games in the postseason, they'd be champions. But their two losses in this run were both at the Boston Garden.

We all figured that Kyrie Irving would come out guns a-blazin' in Game Three. Even if he wouldn't admit it (and he wouldn't), you *know* getting the hell out of Dodge (Boston) would free him up a bit. And, sure enough, Irving came out on fire with nine points in the first eight minutes of play, and the Dallas Mavericks built up a 13-point lead. I've been in enough of these hostile road games (hello, Philadelphia 76ers, Game Six in 1981), and the key is being able to absorb the home team's best shot. The other team is going to come out with all the energy—both from themselves and the crowd.

If you can handle that, it messes with their confidence, like "What else can we do?"

The Green did what it had been doing all season long in situations like this—taking it one play at a time—just like Joe Mazzulla preaches. The Celtics got the lead down to nine, and then a Jayson Tatum three made it a six-point game. A few moments later, Sam Hauser did the same, and it was down to a two-point difference. By the end of the first quarter in a must-win game, when Luka Doncic went off for 13 and Irving for nine, it was just a 31–30 Mavs lead. I *knew* it was over—not just the game but the series, too. "They came out swinging," Jayson Tatum said. "That was to be expected. They were at home, the crowd was behind them. We expected their first punch."

Over the past couple of years, this Celtics team has been ridiculous on the road. *Nothing* fazes them. Down 3–0 to the Miami Heat, they won two must-have games on the road. That was the case even in 2022, when we were down 3–2 to the Milwaukee Bucks. Tatum erupted for 46 in a win at Milwaukee.

And I can relate. I'm not sure why, but I *loved* playing on the road. The guys all felt closer, and we had just one mission. My mission was to make the kids in the front row cry. That's what I wanted to do. Boo-hoo. I loved that, and these Celtics were that team, too. They wanted to send the opposition home and have them with tears in their eyes. There's nothing sweeter than that.

In Game Three in 2024, the Mavericks took a 51–50 lead into the half. I'm sure they thought they were in good shape because they were moving the ball well, kept the Celtics' offense under control, and had only 24 minutes left to get back into the series. But I think deep in their hearts, they were like, *Oh shit! We did all that and we only lead by one!*

The third quarter was all Jaylen Brown. He took over the game and made the statement that "I'm going to be the best player in this series!" He just unleashed a torrent of hurt on Dallas. He dunked, he made threes, then he posted up. You know how all the "experts" said Doncic was the best player in this series? Well, Brown put everyone on notice that this was *his* series and did it in a vintage J.B. way, understated. The guy got it done with 15 points in a 12-minute spurt.

And there was an unlikely contributor as well. Xavier Tillman stepped in for Porzingis and didn't miss a beat. X isn't as talented as K.P.—I mean, we're talking about one of the best big men in the NBA—but Tillman has played a variety of roles during his career. The stat line wouldn't jump out— 11 minutes played, four rebounds, two blocks, and he even hit three-pointer—but the fact that Mazzulla could count on X to be ready for work was huge. His defense on Doncic, which helped tire out the offensive weapon, was key. "They were kind of hinting at potentially if KP's work didn't go well and he didn't feel comfortable, I was going to have to step in," Tillman said. "I feel like switching is like my bread and butter defensively. That's something that allows me to use my quick feet and my strength to be able to kind of bump guys off versus being in a drop coverage and having used my vertical leap. So for me being able to switch and stuff, that is more catered for me. So being able to get subbed in and used for those opportunities, I feel like I can excel the majority of the time."

We outscored them 35–19 in the third quarter. The Mavs tried to come back, cutting it to a one-point deficit with an Irving two, but it wasn't enough, especially when Doncic fouled out with four minutes to go. "We had a good chance," Doncic said. "We were close, just didn't get it. I wish I was out there."

The Celtics handled the scoring runs and momentum swings. "Not really trying to look too much into it," Tatum said. "The game of basketball is about runs. It's never going to go like you expected. If you want to be a champion, you have to be resilient in those situations, and we did that tonight."

"We've been in those moments a lot," Brown added. "And we've been in those positions, and we've lost. It was great to overcome that with my brother, Jayson, and with our team. That was special."

It was time for the fat lady to start warming up. This thing was over.

* * *

This is what Jayson Tatum said before Game Four: "When we were in Dallas and we went up 3–0, oh my God. Nobody has ever come back from 0–3. So I remember getting back to the locker room, and I remember saying, 'I don't know what game it's going to be, but we're going to win the championship.' That was a weird feeling. I wasn't able to sleep that night, and I remember the morning of Game Four we had shootaround, and I had never been in the position that if we win tonight, we're champions."

J.T. could just as well have skipped Game Four to catch up on his sleep because it was *ugly*. In the first quarter, Tatum hit a layup to give the Boston Celtics an 11–10 lead. That was the highlight of the entire night. The guys knew they were playing with house money. The series was over for all intents and purposes. Having already won the road game they needed to take control of the Dallas Mavericks, they took their foot off the pedal.

How bad was it? At the end of the first quarter, Dallas led 34–21. It was the most points the Mavericks had scored in any quarter for the entire series. After 12 minutes Jrue Holiday somehow managed to be -16 and didn't have a single point. The Jays, you ask? Both were -13. This was bad. Somehow, the second quarter was just as awful as the first. By halftime Luka Doncic had already dropped 25 points, and Kyrie Irving had 11. J.T. shot better and had 15 points...to go with a -25 net rating. Holiday was an unfathomable -28. The lead was 26, and it wasn't getting any better.

The final score was 122–84. Tatum was our high scorer with 15 points. He was followed by Sam Hauser with 14 and Payton Pritchard with 11. Nothing against those guys, but that is not a winning formula. It was the third-largest loss in NBA Finals history. As usual, Joe Mazzulla was a man of few words when talking about how his team competed. "It wasn't as good as Dallas' was," he said. "Theirs was a lot better."

And as usual, Jason Kidd wasn't afraid of hurting anyone's feelings. "When you talk about the record or the series is 3–0, somewhere in this game, there's going to be a point where either team is going to have to make a stand or they let go of the rope," he said. "They let go of the rope pretty early."

The Celtics basically threw their shoes out. The other team was capable enough to do what they needed to do. I was totally fine with what happened in Game Four. It wasn't the end of the world. I knew the Celtics would just say, "Okay, we got our ass kicked, and now we have to get back on the horse and start riding again."

It reminded me of what happened to us in Game Six against the Los Angeles Lakers in 1984. We were up 3–2 and we could have won the title in Los Angeles. We had no intention of going back home for a winner-take-all Game Seven. We'd just kicked the Lakers' ass in the sauna known as Boston Garden. (Ask Kareem Abdul-Jabbar, who was sucking from an oxygen mask, about it.) It was time to wrap this up. But Pat Riley was searching for something. He knew his team was dead in the water. He put in a rookie named Byron Scott who dropped 11 points off the bench, and we were all tied at three games apiece.

L.A. definitely poked the bear. James Worthy shoved me into the basket support, and then the fans poured beer on M.L. Carr as we left the floor. We were finishing this bitch at home.

We knew the series should have been over earlier, but "Little Game" James choked away Game Two with an awful pass because he didn't want to go to the free-throw line. Gerald Henderson made the steal and layup, and we had life. We knew—just like this Celtics team—that the highs and lows of the playoffs are so different. To reach the highs, it's like walking up Mount Everest, but when you go down, it's like you're cruising on a bicycle. This was time to take care of business.

My broadcast partner, Sean Grande, threw out the idea that maybe the Celtics were playing a bit of cat and mouse so they could close out the championship on their home floor. I told him that was total bullshit. You put your damn foot on the guy's throat, and you keep it there, especially when you're as hungry as these guys were about winning that championship.

The guys were gracious after getting smoked. They gave credit to their opponent. "Usually, by the second game, you're making adjustments. Third game, you're making another adjustment, and that's kind of how it is," Al Horford said. "And for us we've had the first three games, we didn't really make any adjustments. So today they did something. We have to see what we can, how we can be better, and prepare for it. That's kind of where we're at right now. But it's the playoffs, and they are fighting for their lives, and they played better than us."

The Jays also praised the Mavericks' effort. "You've got to come out and meet their intensity to finish things out. So, we didn't do that tonight. Give credit to Dallas," Jaylen Brown said. "They played extremely well. Those guys, they crashed, they rebounded, and they played with force. Some of those other guys stepped up...We're going to learn from it. We're going to see how and why exactly where the game was won and lost. And then we take those experiences and then we come out and we play like our life depends on it because it does."

"We didn't expect anything to be easy, but it's no reason to lose our head," Tatum said. "Tip your cap to Dallas. They came out and played well, and we've just got to be better on the next one."

I loved the humility but also loved how Holiday can always spin things forward. "It's a great opportunity to respond. Give credit to Dallas," Holiday said. "They came out, and they played with force, and they played great. We just regroup. We keep our same mentality, and we come out and get ready to fight in another battle on our home floor."

We were heading back to Boston, and I knew two things for sure: first, the Celtics would be ready to play in Game Five, and second, I wouldn't want to be the Mavs.

CHAPTER SIXTEEN

A GARDEN CORONATION

You might think our flight home after the beatdown in Game Four would be a real downer. You'd be wrong. The guys were confident. They'd done their job by winning a game in Dallas, were up 3–1, and were ready to wrap things up. The mood was the same jovial mood I'd seen all year. There was a sense of anticipation like the night before Christmas when you're waiting and waiting, knowing that you're going to get the gift you've always wanted, and the time can't go fast enough.

If you have a choice, obviously you'd rather win the title at home. It makes for a storybook ending. Back when we beat the Houston Rockets in 1981, we had to do it in Houston, which was perfectly nice. But when we won at home in 1984 against the Los Angeles Lakers? Now that was mayhem. Michael Cooper pulled up for a meaningless three-pointer (and missed), and then the floodgates just opened up, and it seemed every single fan stormed the floor.

The funny thing is I was able to pretty much avoid the mayhem. After I blocked Coop's shot, I went straight to the exit and beat the crowd's rush to the floor. If you look at the video, you'll see Kareem Abdul-Jabbar getting pummeled, hit with elbows, and throwing elbows in return. Larry Bird was running off the floor, literally punching people to clear his path. It was a different time for sure. Back then, the fans literally lined up in the last minute of the game so they could storm the floor. That ain't happening nowadays. Security is so much tighter; the players never have to worry about it. The court is roped off so the fans can't get to them. (Believe it or not, I have actually had to practice coming out on the floor for presentations a couple of times. It's like a whole rehearsal.) Even with the change in security protocol, there's nothing like winning it on your home floor.

Things were certainly set up perfectly to have that celebration, and I wasn't going to jinx anything. Before each game I always go up to Jayson Tatum and tell him, "You're the baddest motherfucker out here!" But not on this night. I went against routine because I didn't want to tempt fate. We all knew what was about to happen—there was no chance the Dallas Mavericks were coming back—but why take chances?

It was probably nervous energy, but both teams came out ice cold. In the first two minutes and 30 seconds, there was a total of one basket scored. By the end of the first quarter, the Boston Celtics had put together a little run with the Jays and Sam Hauser scoring, and we led by 10 after 12 minutes. This game was starting to take on the same kind of feeling as when the Celtics destroyed L.A. in Game Six of 2008 to win our last title. The Jays had that same aura that Paul Pierce, Kevin Garnett, and Ray Allen did that night. I was impressed with how Tatum came out of the gate. For all the noise about his poor shooting, J.T. did a little bit of everything. By halftime he already had 16 points, nine assists, and four boards.

But there were two things that were so memorable from that first half. Kristaps Porzingis had essentially talked his way into the lineup after missing the previous two games. Of course, his impact wasn't the same as when he jumped off the bench in Game One—that was a once-in-a-lifetime moment—and it was clear that K.P. was compromised, but like he said, someone would have had to kill him for him to miss this opportunity. He only scored five points in 16 minutes, but as his coach pointed out, this was about way more than numbers. "That was awesome. It's a huge credit to him," Joe Mazzulla said. "I know he's been in and out in the playoffs, but he's worked his ass off to try and get in and play as much as he could. And even though he wasn't 100 percent, he said he wanted to play and he knew he could give us something. And I thought that the minutes he gave us were valuable. It speaks to who he is, and it speaks to the locker room."

To be honest, I didn't love the idea of K.P. playing once I saw him come out on the floor because he looked so limited. We have such a great coaching and medical staff who know what they're doing, but you don't normally take those chances. Maybe it was something different because you're about to win a championship, but I think the Celtics were going to win it with or without him at that point. So I probably would have said, "Dude, you're not going out there" because you could see he was already limping.

The Dallas Mavericks were smart and attacked Porzingis every chance they could. He couldn't move, and they were fighting for their lives. Don't get me wrong—I trust our medical staff, but I would have erred on the side of caution. I've always heard the Celtics take it out of the player's hands in a case like this. We aren't back in the 1980s, where there would have been peer pressure, "Well, you gonna play? What you gonna do?" The way the league is today, everybody would have understood if he hadn't come out on the floor at all. I get that every player wants to be out there and try to help their team, but if you look back at it now, there was probably more of a chance of him making things worse based on how he was limping along.

K.P.'s return was inspirational, but there was one specific play that nobody will ever forget. Back in the deciding game of 2008, Garnett made a ridiculous drive to the paint, waited until Lamar Odom came down, drew the foul, and banked it home to give the Celtics a 21-point lead. This was like déjà vu all over again.

At the end of Game Two, Payton Pritchard thrilled the fans with a three-pointer from just inside of halfcourt to end the third quarter. That was cool. In Game Five he went a step farther—or literally several steps farther. The Celtics were up by 18 and well on their way to title No. 18. Luka Doncic missed a free throw, Al Horford grabbed the board, and then gave it to Pritchard, who drilled the three...from 49 feet! It was the longest shot in the Finals since 1998, and the crowd just lost its mind.

As usual, Mazzulla knew exactly what he was doing by putting P.P. in the ballgame. "Payton is one of the best competitors and one of my favorite people in the world. Just the way he competes, the professionalism, and just for his ability to take pride in stuff like that," said Mazzulla, who was talking about a guy who on some nights doesn't even get off the bench. "He won us moments. As the playoffs go on, obviously some patterns change, and things change, but those guys have to win moments of games for you, and Payton did that twice for us. That is just as important as any other plays that happened throughout the series and in the playoffs alone. I've got a huge heart for him."

It turns out that Mazzulla wasn't the one who had planned this all out. Pritchard and Horford had talked things through ahead of time. "It was funny because before the game," Horford said, "when we were talking about how many dribbles you could take or how many seconds you have, [how] many dribbles you can potentially take. And we were talking about it, I was like, 'Well, just to be safe, don't overdribble.'"

He certainly didn't. It was just one dribble, a little shuffle of the feet, and then destiny. "In the moment I just feel like I have deep range," Pritchard said. "And if I can find a spot that I can get it there, I just believe...I guess that's the secret."

The box score shows that Pritchard only played one minutes, 25 second in the game, but nobody will ever forget what he did. You could see the look on the Mavericks' faces. Stick a fork in them...they were done.

The second half was basically one long coronation. I just knew that Tatum was going to have a good game because I could feel the pressure that he had pent up for all those years. You could compare his clinching game (31 points, 11 assists, and eight rebounds) to my Game Seven against the Lakers (24, eight, eight), but there were some differences. By 1984 I had already won a title and was named Finals MVP. Plus, I literally *hated* the Lakers, especially James Worthy, who had cheap-shotted me. J.T. hadn't reached the promised land yet.

Although I don't know that he loved Dallas, he was out there dapping guys up before the game. I can tell you there was no way we were doing that with the Fakers. He just had a sense of: "I'm out here and I'm going to do some damage."

With less than a minute to go, Tatum—the guy who doesn't show emotion—broke down on the sidelines, sobbing with his head in his hands. I think it all just hit him at that moment.

He and Joe embraced, with J.T. shouting, "I told you so! I told you so!"

Here's what Mazzulla said led to that emotional outburst. "There's another level of commitment to winning that we have to make, and we would always talk," he said. "You have to make this level of commitment to winning. You have to surrender to the fact that you could lose it all, but you have to have the ultimate faith that you're going to win. And that moment was kind of a culmination of that. We talked a lot about it in a couple of years of you have to feel like it's your time. You have to surrender to the fact that you could give up everything for success and lose, but you got to trust that if you commit to the process of winning, your chances of winning are better."

As a broadcaster you always wonder what you'll say in the big moment. My radio partner, Sean Grande, was totally prepared. "The 2024 Boston Celtics are one of the greatest teams in NBA history," he said in the final seconds. "They were told they had to win. There's only one thing you can do when expectations are that high—meet them. And there's only one way to stop being haunted by the ghosts and the legends and champions inside this building—join them. Together they have and together they stand alone on top of the mountain for now. And once again the Boston Celtics stand alone for all time. It is banner 18. The mission demanded is mission accomplished."

People have asked me why I was so quiet in that final minute. *Was I overcome?* No, not really. *Was I taking in the moment?* Yeah, I was. Winning a championship is so rare that I wanted to see everything that was happening. But there was another reason for my silence: I had to pee! NBC Sports Boston's star reporter, Abby Chin, had told me about a game she filled in for me on the radio, and as Grande was talking about something, she just blurted out that she needed to hit the bathroom. I may not have announced it, but *that* was my reason.

* * *

To see the looks from the Jays, Al Horford, Derrick White, etc. was so cool. It was different from when my teams won; we got our first title in Larry Bird's second season. These guys had been so close for so long that this was relief and pure joy. "To be able to say we did it, that we came together, and we won a championship. Banner No. 18 has been hanging over our head for so many years," Jayson Tatum said through the tears. "To know that we're going to be engraved in history, and it still hasn't like registered. I'm just still trying to process it all."

For the guys on this team that lost a couple of years earlier—on their home floor—to the Golden State Warriors, well, this was as sweet as it gets. "Coming up short and having failures makes this moment that much better," Tatum said. "You know what it feels like to be on the other side of this and be in the locker room and hearing the other team celebrate on your home floor. That was devastating."

Jaylen Brown reflected on the moment. "We learned from all of our mistakes," Brown said. "All of our adversity has made us stronger, made us tougher. All season you could see it. We started from the jump. We made all the sacrifices. We played both ends of the ball at a high level. We didn't skip any steps. And this was the result."

In a really cool gesture, Tatum gave shoutouts to former teammates Marcus Smart and Robert Williams. I can only imagine what it was like for Smart, who was the longest-tenured player in Boston, to see his guys win without him. He tweeted out congratulations and then appeared on a podcast with Theo Pinson and spilled it all out, saying it was bittersweet. "I know everybody's expecting me to be salty and shit, but there's no hard feelings for them. Don't get it twisted," Smart said. "It's definitely tough because I was in the trenches with them. So, to not be able to finish what you started with those guys is definitely tough. But, man, shit, my wife will tell you, I was screaming for those guys when they won just as much as anybody else because I have love for those guys and I know the work that they put in. And I've been through it."

It would have been really easy for the guy, who said he let the whole city down after Game Seven against the Miami Heat the previous year, to tell everyone to eat it, but instead J.B. used his (and the team's) failures to make everyone stronger. "All of those experiences led to here," he said. "All of those moments where we came up short, we felt like we let the city down, let ourselves down, all of that compiled is how we get to this moment."

It wasn't just the Jays either. This group fit together as well as just about any team I've seen. When they needed a big three-pointer, you knew someone was going to step up and get it. The coach had his finger right on the pulse of his players. "You can't have a philosophy or a way of playing if you don't have a group of guys that are willing to buy into it and be disciplined," Joe Mazzulla said. "Quite honestly, this group of guys has been through so much in the league. They know what it takes."

Not only did they play well, but they also played for each other. "I hope that when people watch us play, they see the joy that we play with," Jrue Holiday said. "We love playing together, and we got it done together."

As for the team president, well, his mind was already racing forward. "My whole background is as a coach," Brad Stevens told NBA TV as confetti filled the air. "Coaches never feel good. We were in there just watching all these guys spraying champagne, and I'm like, 'How the hell are we going to play in our first game next year?' So, I think that that's just the way that you think."

At the postgame ceremony, I (thankfully) wasn't asked to present the MVP trophy. After the Eastern Conference Finals debacle, I was 100 percent good with that. The Bill Russell MVP award certainly could have gone to Tatum, especially after his huge Game Five, but Brown snagged the honor, which I definitely agree with. For a guy who had been overlooked so often in his career, I couldn't be happier. J.B. was overcome with emotion. "To be honest, I can't even put it into words. Just Bill

Russell and what he's meant for me through my Boston journey and his spirit, everything that he stood for, just for this to be the Bill Russell MVP Award, it just…I've got nothing, man. I don't even know what to say. It's unreal. I can't even put into words the emotions," Brown said. "My teammates were great. They allowed me to lead us on both ends of ball, and we just came out and performed on our home floor. It's just amazing."

But before Brown was done, he had a special shoutout to his running mate. "It could have gone to anybody. It could have gone to Jayson. Jayson, I can't talk enough about his self-lessness," Brown said. "I can't talk enough about his attitude. It's just how he approached not just this series or the Finals but just the playoffs in general. And we did it together as a team, and that was the most important thing."

* * *

In today's media world, everyone has a hot take. That's not exactly breaking news, but what some of the people said still boggles my mind. Shaquille O'Neal did a podcast with Udonis Haslem and Mike Miller—two former members of the Miami Heat, who, of course, were bitter rivals of the Boston Celtics. Haslem made headlines during both the Eastern Conference Finals and NBA Finals by saying that Jayson Tatum was jealous when Jaylen Brown won MVP in both series. That's total BS in my opinion. Shaq got on *The OGs Show* and took a shot at the Celtics. "We all know Boston had the easiest run ever to that championship," he said. Of, course his former Heat teammates agreed. Then Shaq added, "Can they back it up?"

What a crock. They then talked about how Donovan Mitchell missed two games in the second round with a strained calf, and Tyrese Haliburton missed the last two games in the Eastern Conference Finals with a bad hamstring. The Athletic did a study showing that in terms of missed games by All-Stars, Boston had the easiest path to a title of any team in the past 25 years.

I have a few thoughts on this. First, should the Celtics have not played those games? Maybe wait until everyone is healthy for the opposition? You play who is in front of you, and that's that. But as veteran sportswriter Bob Ryan points out, facts are facts. "They're going to have to live with it until they win it a second time because it was just an incredible fact that Mitchell got hurt, and Haliburton was hurt, and Butler was hurt," said Ryan before noting that this could be a positive. "They played these people when they were not at 100 percent. And it's given people a reason to question their validity, which actually is going to turn out to be another motivating thing, I think. And that's fine, *we'll show you*. This is going to be the we'll-show-you team."

Secondly, as *The Boston Globe* writer Gary Washburn and I discussed on *my* podcast, did Shaq notice that Kristaps Porzingis only played in seven of the team's 19 playoff games? And my friend Wash—who grew up a Los Angeles Lakers fan—pointed out in Shaq and Kobe Bryant's three-peat, they beat a Philadelphia 76ers team with Hall of Famers Allen Iverson and Dikembe Mutombo but little else, an Indiana Pacers team with Reggie Miller and a bunch of "guys," and a Brooklyn Nets team led by Jason Kidd and a roster of people you'd never remember. Back in those days, the Eastern Conference was considered a joke, and all of the really good teams—like the Portland Trail Blazers, San Antonio Spurs, and Sacramento Kings—were in the West. Not exactly a murderers' row, is it?

Wash also points out that when we won in 1981, everyone—including us—was sure we'd be going up against the Lakers. But Moses Malone had other ideas, and the Houston Rockets knocked out the defending champions in the first round. We ended up beating the 40–42 Rockets—that's right; they got to the Finals with a losing record—in six games. Why don't you ask me if we want to give back the championship trophy, or if I don't consider myself the real playoff MVP?

Injuries are always going to be a factor in sports. Ryan also points out that during the 1958 Finals, Bill Russell injured his ankle, which combined with a historic performance by Bob Pettit, led to the St. Louis Hawks' only championship. He also cites Porzingis' injury as a fair retort and the fact that the Celtics had the most 20-point leads of any team in NBA history for one season. Oh, and they went 16–3 during the playoffs. And as far as Shaq? "That's fine," Ryan said. "I mean, he's a Laker at heart. He's never gone, even though he did give the Celtics a little cursory service, not much."

Haters gonna hate, and Jrue Holiday knows that the universal praise is short-lived. "People see us at the top of the mountain now. I think last year they kind of saw that, too," he said. "We've heard good and bad. Honestly, I think it's going to be the same thing. People are going to say that we suck, and other people will think we're really good."

CHAPTER SEVENTEEN

JAYSON TATUM

When you look at what Jayson Tatum has accomplished in his career, people should be floored. Five-time All-Star, four-time All-NBA (the last three years have been first-team), three consecutive top six finishes in the MVP race, and, of course, now, NBA champion and two-time Olympic gold medal winner. But it's crazy to me how much shit this guy takes. In the championship run, there was so much talk about him not being clutch. Give. Me. A. Break. In 2022 with his team trailing 3–2 and playing at Milwaukee, J.T. went for 46 points against the Bucks. Oh, by the way, in that season's Eastern Conference Finals, he averaged 25 points and won the Larry Bird Trophy as series MVP.

He's never been in the news for doing anything wrong and has been the best player on the best team in the East for most of his career. But all we ever hear about is what he *can't* do.

Look at last year's Finals. Did he shoot well? Not at all—39 percent from the floor and 26 percent from three. I think the shooting got in his head for a minute because he remembered what happened with the Golden State Warriors. I do believe that was one of the things that he actually looked at and thought about. And it did affect him, but he was able to bounce back. To use a golf analogy, the thing that he did differently this time was he went to the other clubs. The driver wasn't working; so, he went to the short game. If the shot wasn't going, he was going to be rebounding, he was going to be a facilitator. He was going to set the table in that way. And that's what made this team better. He didn't just hang his head. Sure, it would have been easy to turtle in the corner and let Jaylen Brown do the heavy lifting. But that's not J.T.

No—quite the contrary—he pulled down nearly eight boards and dished out seven assists a game and played his customary stellar defense. Oh, and he went for 31 points, 11 assists, and eight rebounds in the clinching game to lead his team to a title. He had let his poor shooting affect his game in the Finals against Golden State. When it wasn't going, the other parts of his game went to shit. That wasn't going to happen this time around.

In my opinion the reason the Celtics won this year was because Tatum allowed Brown to be Batman while he played the role of Robin. It reminds me of our 1981 title, which was Larry Bird's first. Did anyone possibly think that Bird would let me be Batman? *Hell no, it's Larry Bird!* But that's what great teams do. They're able to see a guy, who is scoring and doing things well, and they keep feeding that guy. You might not get the individual fame, but you win the championship. In 1984 we had four Hall of Famers, but when they saw I had it going on, they just kept on feeding me, and I took us to the promised land.

And here's a cool note about how "bad" Tatum was in the Finals. He became just the sixth player in NBA history to lead his team in points, rebounds, and assists in the playoffs while winning the title. The other guys were pretty damn good: Larry Bird, Tim Duncan, Hakeem Olajuwon, LeBron James, and Nikola Jokic. That's 13 MVP awards and 15 NBA championships. Three of them are in the Hall of Fame, and James and the Joker are certain to join them after they retire.

How many teams would kill to have a player like this? "He had a great closeout game, right? He's a special player. And look: defenses are geared toward him and forcing him to pass," assistant general manager Austin Ainge said. "We had kind of a just a crazy year where we won so many games both in the regular season and the playoffs that [the media] get bored and nitpick things."

Even with the full support of management, the coaching staff, and his teammates, J.T. sill heard the noise. "It's tough to see people talking about you on TV or doubting you on TV or all the things they say on Twitter because," he said, "for one, how much you sacrifice and how hard you work on your craft…You want to be the best. You want to play your best every single night, and it just doesn't work out that way."

Tatum's maturity is really something to behold. Brown was the guy who was hot. J.T. didn't force the issue. He didn't bitch. He didn't complain. He took his shots. He played his role. They won the championship. Before the 2024 NBA Finals, Kendrick Perkins went on ESPN and put this out there: "I'm so over Jayson Tatum. When is he going to arrive? He talked about how he couldn't wait to get to the postseason. Well, it's here. What are you going to do about it? It's in his hands; this is Jayson Tatum's moment."

Brad Stevens has been with Tatum every step of the way, and he honestly could not care less about what the talking heads like Perk say. "I want to be as respectful as I can when I say this, but who cares about the criticism? And then when you think about why people would ever criticize him, and you realize that their job is paid to give an opinion that I'm not sure even they agree with most of the time," Stevens said. "I've heard Jayson say this: if they're talking about you, it means you're pretty damn good. And that's real. But Jayson's got good competitive character. I don't think any of us have ever worried about his ability to handle the noise."

Stevens told The Ringer, "There are a lot of things in this job that I lose sleep over. What someone thinks about Jayson Tatum, or Jayson Tatum playing well is not one."

One of the best traits about the two Jays is their self-confidence. Both guys refuse to give critics any power—or for that matter—any space in their heads. Instead Tatum praised the fans who supported him. "There's a lot of people that doubted us, and I remember thinking about, *Man, when we win the championship, I can't wait to tell everybody that doubted us, that had something to say,*" J.T. said. "But you realize that moment that we won, when the confetti was falling and then the parade, it's not about the people that doubted you. It's about you guys, the guys that supported us along the way."

When J.T. came to Boston, he walked into a team that had guys like Kyrie Irving, Al Horford, Marcus Smart, and, of course, a second-year player named Jaylen Brown. (Gordon Hayward was injured five minutes into the season and didn't play again that year.) That's a lot of mouths to feed and a lot of strong personalities. Oh, and Tatum was all of 19 years old!

As you can imagine, he was very, very quiet and laid back. Watching him do an interview now is like night and day. He's still not the in-your-face kind of guy, but now he's not afraid to show his personality. Before he was extremely guarded, and now he's pulled the curtain back a little bit. It's very cool to see his evolution and the fact is that he's only 27. As great as he's been on and off the court, I think he's just scratching the surface.

After the criticism Tatum faced in the Finals, he probably figured he was pretty much home free. The Celtics had finally won the title, he was about to get the biggest contract in NBA history, and he was heading to Paris for his second Olympics. But J.T. showed incredible maturity in the face of adversity. At Media Day in September, he even joked about how Joe Mazzulla was probably thrilled that he didn't win Finals MVP and sat out two of the games during the Olympics. Mazzulla responded that Jayson was 100 percent right. "I mean, that's just the way that I love him," Mazzulla said. "And the relationship that we have, I appreciate that he accepts my perspective and the way that we go about talking about it."

If anyone earned a break after an incredibly long season and summer, it would be Tatum.

But that's not how truly great players become greater. In the heat of the moment, J.T. knew it wasn't time for any drastic changes. The team was in the survive-and-advance mode. "Yeah, I mean, there's some things I could have fixed," he said. "But just in the midst of the playoffs and trying to manage your rest and things like that, it's a little tough."

Now after the championship and Olympics, the lab was open during the dog days of summer. "[We'd] watch a lot of film work," he said, "been working with my trainer, Drew, a lot recently [on a] few mechanical things, pick-up points, hand placement, getting lower, keeping my shoulders forward, and things like that."

* * *

From Jayson Tatum's perspective, he knows if the team eats, he eats. "I'm not the only superstar to not win Finals MVP," he told TNT. "Steph Curry got four rings, and he only has one. Isiah Thomas didn't win every time. Larry Bird didn't win Finals MVP every time he won a championship. The most important part is that we won, and I know I played a huge role in us winning a championship…I know that I'm going to win Finals MVP one day, which means I get to win another championship."

Tatum has an old soul. He does a really good job of keeping everything in perspective, and for someone his age, that's pretty incredible. Over the years he's developed a friendship with Bill Russell's widow, Jeannine. So you can imagine how meaningful it was when a few months after Bill's death, she spoke with J.T. "I remember her telling me how much he enjoyed watching us play and how proud of me he was and how much he supported us even later in his life," Tatum said. "Even when he wasn't as talkative, he could still watch and see things. She just kept saying how proud of us that he was."

If the Jays retired today, they wouldn't be on the Mount Rushmore of all-time great Boston Celtics like Russell. Not yet anyway. I wouldn't put Jaylen Brown there right now either as one of the all-timers because he's just scratching the surface. Tatum, on the other hand, is closer to knocking on the door because of his consistency over the last several years and being first-team All-NBA the past three years. It's not like we're talking about the Los Angeles Clippers after all. These are the *18-time champion Celtics!*

I mean, you have to start with Russell. A lot of people think Larry Bird is the greatest Celtics player, and he *is* one of the best players in NBA history. But Russell won two championships in college, an Olympic gold, then 11 NBA titles—including eight in a row! Oh, and for his last one, he coached *and* played. Needless to say, Russell is on any Mount Rushmore.

Another easy one, of course, is Bird. You've got to include John Havlicek. He's one of the all-time greats. I'm not sure how you can keep Kevin McHale off the list. So, unless we redo Rushmore and make it with 10 presidents, I can't put Tatum in there yet. Maybe one day but not now.

I'm so impressed with Tatum's respect for those who came before him. We had always been good since the time he came into the league. But one day I walked into the locker room, and I heard, "Cornbread, Cornbread, you were a bad motherfucker!"

Tatum had just watched *Best of Enemies*, an ESPN 30 for 30 documentary about our battles with the Los Angeles Lakers. He told me he thought I was just the guy who did radio but didn't know anything about my career. Him learning that was one of the coolest things I've had happen to me.

Not to sound like the old man telling kids to get off my lawn, but this generation of players generally don't know the history of the game. Nobody is ever going to just blurt out that Sam Jones was one of the best shooters of all time, but he was. I always appreciate it when guys like Tatum pay homage to the older players. "Larry Bird is the best Celtic to ever wear this uniform, and that's the guy that I'm chasing," Tatum said. "Even if I fall short of that, if I aspire to be as great as he was and if you fall a little short, you had a hell of a career. My motivation is to chase the best players to ever play, the best players to ever wear a Celtic uniform."

That's music to his coach's ears. "I just said, 'Listen, you've accomplished so much in this league and just take a step back and appreciate that,'" Joe Mazzulla said. "But then be grateful that you've got God-willing 10, 12, 14 years left in this league. Who knows what you're going to see?' And I don't think we've seen the best of him yet in terms of how much he works and how he's got something to work for."

And one of the things I like best about J.T. is his self-awareness. Tatum knows he's not a finished project. "I'm only 26. I played a lot of basketball so far. So, I've still got a long way to go, a lot of basketball left, a lot of things I can get better at," Tatum told *The Boston Globe*. "I can tweak and be more effective and efficient in things and impactful and finding different ways to dominate the game. I feel like that's my challenge night to night."

CHAPTER EIGHTEEN

JAYLEN BROWN

When the Boston Celtics announced Jaylen Brown as the third overall pick in the 2016 NBA Draft, it was loudly booed by the fans. They wanted a trade for Jimmy Butler or Paul George—not a guy who most fans were unaware of in his one year at the University of California. But Brown's motivation came even before the draft. He tells a story about a high school teacher telling him that he was destined for Cobb County (Georgia) jail. "In Georgia the education system isn't the best; so, I don't really put too much blame on the teacher," Brown told Boston.com. "It is what it is. When you have one teacher handling 35 kids in one class, it's tough. A lot of teachers go through stuff and take a lot of crap out there all day. So who knows what was going through her mind that day when she said that."

After initially brushing that comment aside, Brown did not: "When someone says something like that, you never really forget it."

Think about that for a second. Now if that's not motivation for you to go out and slap somebody in the face, I don't know what is. I would love for him just to go back and see that particular teacher. I would love to know what that teacher's name was. Like how did the teacher get there? What did you see that was so freaking bad? But to me that was more of a motivational factor. Even when there were doubters from the outside, Brown wasn't going to let them win. "I just came in and kept my head down and told myself, *I'm going to just keep working,*" he said. "To be here in this moment now through all the years, through all the doubt, through all of the ups and downs, through all of the verdicts, through all of the everything, it just makes the story that much sweeter."

There's no question that J.B. has a chip on his shoulder. "I've had to experience a lot of adversity—through life, through this organization, through my journey," he said. "A lot of people, a lot of doubts, a lot of ins and outs to get to where I'm at. I'm grateful. I wouldn't exchange it for anything because even in those moments of doubts or I heard boos—people wanted me gone. They didn't think I deserved what I got, that kind of made me who I was."

It's kind of a what-doesn't-kill-you-makes-you-stronger mind-set for J.B. "We often look at blessings as being something positive, but all the blessings in my life have been the adversity and the negative things that have happened," he said, "like being benched early, getting the short end of the stick. We had a bunch of guys early in my career. There's been a lot of stuff. All of those moments I look back on, it added to my demeanor, my mind-set, and where I am now."

* * *

When the Boston Celtics struggled to start the 2018 season, ESPN's Jackie MacMullan wrote a bombshell story describing Jaylen Brown's discontent. She retold a story about Marcus Smart pleading J.B. to wake up. "Hey!" he barked at

Brown. "We're here for you. We want to help. We want to hear from you."

Silence from Brown ensued.

"Say something!" Smart said. "Participate with us! Are you with us?"

Now the quiet Brown didn't have his best season, but he obviously bounced back in a huge way. The way that he's improved each and every season reminds Bob Ryan of perhaps the greatest Celtics player of them all—Larry Joe Bird. After we got swept in 1983 by the Milwaukee Bucks, Ryan spoke with Bird in the locker room. "Larry said that he was going to go home and work on his game, he's going to come back, it's going to be better. And damn it he comes back with this throw shot from the corner that he didn't have," Ryan said. "Going to half, jump, half hook, turn around, and he worked on his left even more."

On the court Brown has an innate ability to just get better and to work hard; he's got huge motivation, unreal confidence. What's cool about him is that he's also not afraid to work on things he knows he has to get better at. I would see him every day at shootaround or practice with six or seven coaches working on every possession, every spacing imaginable so he could improve his reads. J.B. is the poster child for the organization's "culture of improvement," as Brad Stevens calls it. "Jaylen just started at a different place because physically he's so gifted, and there was so much expectation when he was younger," Stevens said. "He's a far different, better player than when he first got here. I think the annual commitment to and daily commitment to improving has been very evident."

This is a guy whose feet are planted where he's at, and J.B. is certainly comfortable in his skin. Before Game Two of the Eastern Conference Finals, Brown acknowledged as much when he was asked about not being named All-NBA. "I watch guys get praised and anointed who I feel is half as talented as me on either side of the ball. But at this point in my life, I just embrace it," he said. "It comes with being who I am and what I stand for, and I ain't into changing that. So, I just come out, and I'm grateful to step out on to the floor each and every night and put my best foot forward and get better each year. Whether people appreciate it or not, it is what it is."

I think one of the biggest developments with the championship team is that Brown didn't take a backseat to Jayson Tatum. It was so important to what they were trying to accomplish because it brought a whole new level of competition. One of my issues in years past is that I'd never seen a successful team that doesn't have a guy who goes toe-to-toe with someone else when they're pissed off. The championship season was the first year where I saw Brown step up into that role. He was like, "If you wanna go, we can do whatever needs to be done." There were many times where J.B. went up to players on the opposing team and challenged them. Especially without Marcus Smart, the Celtics needed that.

As great as he is *on* the court, I think J.B. is even more impressive off of it. He has a firm belief of who he is. He carries himself in a unique way. I had the chance to chat with his mother, Mechalle. She gave me more of an understanding of who he is. In fact, when I heard Stephen A. Smith talk trash about Brown, saying that people don't like him, and that's why he isn't getting endorsements, etc., I spoke with Mechalle. She really put it perfectly—her son only moves when he has a cause. If he doesn't feel it's the right thing to do, he ain't moving.

At the team's victory parade, Brown wore a shirt directed at Smith, saying "State Your Source." That's Brown. At the parade he lost a ring that was crusted in diamonds, saying "7uice." Two fans found it. So not only did J.B. give the fans floor tickets to Opening Night for the championship ring presentation as a thank you, but he also personally delivered the tickets and an autographed basketball—much to the fans' shock and delight.

Maybe the fact that Brown speaks his mind cost him a spot on the Olympic team, but you know what? A championship ring, being named MVP of the Eastern Conference Finals and NBA Finals...oh, and a contract worth more than $300 million? That's a pretty decent consolation prize, I'd say.

That contract came at an odd time—right after the disaster against the Miami Heat in Game Seven of the Eastern Conference Finals. Brown had earned a supermax deal as a result of being named second team All-NBA. To be honest, I wasn't necessarily convinced that he should be the highest-paid player in the history of the league (a title that Tatum now holds), but I knew the Celtics needed to keep him.

Ironically, it was that awful Heat series that gave management conviction—not pause. "When we lost Game Three, got just destroyed in Miami to go down 3–0, it looked like we were dead in the water," Stevens said. "I rode the second bus back to the hotel. We have three buses, and usually I ride the first just to get out of there. But I waited for the second because I wanted to sit with a guy or two. I just wanted to kind of hear what they were thinking and just kind of feel it and be there to lend an ear or whatever. I sat next to Jaylen, and Jaylen just was really hurt. He was really determined not to let this be the end of the story. It was really clear that we were going to be hard to beat in Game Four if everybody had his mind-set, and I thought that he and our team showed great resolve in coming back in that series, though we came up short."

Now that he's a champion, Brown is even more aware of the fact that he's in the spotlight. He still keeps to himself a fair amount, but he did make the rounds after the title, including a trip to Los Angeles for the ESPY Awards, where he won for Best Championship Performance. He knows that everyone is watching him. Even when he attended the NBA Summer League in Las Vegas, he caused a bit of a stir when he was courtside and caught apparently saying "I don't think he's a pro" about Bronny James.

But who Brown is as a man impresses me the most. He got the $304 million deal and right away gave back to his community. J.B. says he wants to create a Black Wall Street in Boston with the idea of trying to at least narrow the financial gap between the haves and have-nots. His first step was to launch Boston Xchange, which is a nonprofit group designed to generate $5 billion in communities of color. This will offer mentoring, coaching, and, of course—money—to help minority startups succeed. "It will be a hub for diverse creators and entrepreneurs," Brown told *The Boston Globe*. "It will operate kind of at the intersection between business and culture. I believe that when you invest in the creator and the culture it strengthens entire cities."

Boston mayor Michelle Wu issued a statement saying: "Jaylen has been changing the game on and off the court, and we are so blessed in Boston to partner with him once again—now with his visionary leadership setting a national standard for innovation and wealth creation. Boston XChange is an example of what's possible when we work together with urgency to create opportunities connecting creators and entrepreneurs to sustainable wealth building that helps our entire community thrive."

And all of this comes after J.B. started The 7uice Foundation, which is designed to help bridge the opportunity for young people of color. I love Brown as a player, but what he's doing off the court may be even more impressive.

CHAPTER NINETEEN

THE JAYS

One of the most remarkable things about Jaylen Brown and Jayson Tatum aka "the Jays" is how long the Boston Celtics kept them together before winning the title. That just doesn't happen in the NBA. As a comparison Michael Jordan and Scottie Pippen only had to wait four years before winning their first of six championships in 1991 for the Chicago Bulls. The Detroit Pistons' Isiah Thomas and Joe Dumars had to wait for their fifth year as teammates. Los Angeles Lakers Magic Johnson and James Worthy won in their third year together.

Patience isn't usually a virtue in NBA front offices. Although so much of the outside noise was about breaking up the Jays, Brad Stevens—first as a coach, then as team president—knew what he had. "Those golden picks from Brooklyn turned out to be Jaylen and Jayson, which Danny absolutely nailed. And so for us, I don't think we ever lost sight of the fact that those guys were super special and unique," Stevens said. "We got them at the right time. I mean, we talked at length about trying to get as many wings as possible so that you could play an interchangeable and switchy game. I think that that's just kind of the way I look at it is: okay, we have these two amazing young players…We have a foundation and to get as many cracks at it with that foundation as possible but also knowing that those guys are going to be your two central guys. You're always going to be in the mix. I think that's a great place to start."

The Jays were together for *seven* long years before reaching the promised land. You'd better believe they celebrated finally breaking through—together. "We've been through a lot, the losses, the expectations. The media have said all different types of things: we can't play together, we are never going to win," Brown said. "We heard it all. But we just blocked it out and we just kept going. I trusted him, he trusted me, and we did it together. To get to this point and share that experience with J.T. is just awesome."

And even though the media tried to portray jealousy between the two, Tatum made clear that none of the outside noise mattered. "The main goal for us was to win a championship. We didn't care who got Finals MVP. I know that I need him through this journey, and he needs me," he said. "It was great to see him have that moment and share that moment with him. I'm extremely happy for him. Well-deserved. That was big time. He earned that."

That's why it was so dumb when longtime Miami Heat player Udonis Haslem went on ESPN and tried to say that J.T. wasn't happy and was even jealous of J.B. winning the Eastern Conference Finals MVP. "Like I wasn't happy for him?" Tatum said incredulously. "Most stars don't make a conference finals until they are 27, 28…We were doing it when we were 19, 20."

Their coach doesn't think it's right to look at one guy vs. another. "I think [it's unfair] being compared to each other," Mazzulla said. "They're different. And you see other duos around the league don't have to go through that, and it's because of the platform that they have. It's because they've been so successful their entire careers. They've been able to [sustain] success at a high level."

These two guys are always going to be linked, and when it comes to individual honors, sometimes one will get the honor; other times it will be the other, and they genuinely don't seem to care. Like in the 2019–20 season, it was coming down to J.T. vs. J.B. for a single All-Star berth. Tatum earned the spot. "And I knew he was happy for me," Tatum said. "But when you are a competitor, you want what's in front of you."

And, of course, Tatum wanted to win MVP in the Eastern Conference and NBA Finals. When Brown took home both, J.T. said he was "genuinely happy." Tatum still leads in individual honors, and for the most part, he's been No. 1 with Brown as the 1A. Coming into this season, J.T. led J.B. in All-Star appearances and All-NBA teams.

Everyone saw in the 2024 postseason just how good Brown can be, but his teammate already knew. "I feel like he has gotten a short end of the stick, whether it's All-Star selections or All-NBA," Tatum said. "I feel like he in a sense made up for some of those shortcomings that people didn't vote him for. I was happy that he got it."

Following Brown's MVP performance against the Indiana Pacers, he stressed the four-letter word: T-E-A-M. "It could have gone to anybody. It could have gone to Jayson. Jayson, like I can't talk enough about his selflessness," Brown said. "I can't talk enough about his attitude. It's just how he approached not just this series or the Finals but just the playoffs in general. And we did it together as a team, and that was the most important thing."

Yeah, Udonis, it really sounds like these two guys don't get along, right?

That's not to say there weren't growing pains. When you have two alpha wings, it's not as easy as, say, a point guard and a center. Tatum acknowledged as much, showing that their maturity is what led them to this title. "We've figured out that we need each other. We have learned how to coexist. And we know we need to be the best version of ourselves in order for all of this to work," he said, adding that he knows their teammates are watching. "We weren't necessarily the best playmakers early in our careers, but we developed into guys that really bleed the game. We want to be a great example of guys that play on both ends of the floor and guys who are the best teammates that we can be."

The sum is even better than its parts. I learned that pretty quickly when Larry Bird came to town. I thought I was the shit, scoring nearly 20 a game and leading the NBA in field-goal percentage, but then I saw Bird in our first practice. Things were going to be different around here. With Robert Parish and Kevin McHale, it was the same thing. Put either of them on most teams, and either would be the go-to guy, maybe even win an MVP. But we all knew Bird was the best player. As soon as we figured that out, we started to win right away.

The biggest difference this year was they had that mean spirit. There were even a couple of times when they started shit on their own. Think about teams that have won the title.

They've all had at least one guy who is a *bad* man. The poster child obviously is Draymond Green.

Now I don't want the Jays to go *that* far, but I do think moving forward you may even see a little more of that. As you mature, you take on a little bit more.

During the championship year, we finally saw the Jays going back at other players. That was a major difference from years past. One time J.T. turned around and started walking up on his opponent. It was a heartbeat steal; like my heartbeat was actually going to come out of my chest. I was so happy and proud. And J.B. just got to be public enemy No. 1. He's making nasty plays. Believe me: that propels his team.

Celtics management has never considered this J.T.'s or J.B.'s team. "Just a terrible narrative that isn't real, I don't think that that's real for any, any team. Not for Michael Jordan, not for Bill Russell, and not for LeBron James. Nobody wins alone," Austin Ainge said.

"Everybody needs everybody, and you need good players to win, and I think our guys are mature enough to know that. And whatever people want to label things, we have run different plays for guys at the end of games...You know all the media narratives I just think are mostly garbage, and we try to avoid them at all costs."

The other media narrative was that the Jays were somehow failures because they'd only gotten to the Finals once (and blew a 2–1 series lead) and kept getting knocked out in the Eastern Conference Finals. Some of the fanbase was getting fed up, but as Ainge points out, you need to look at the big picture. "Through age 25 the success that those guys had, we knew that their primes were still coming up. So, we did not view this as some big failure of their early part of their career. The exact opposite—we were amazed at the success," he said. "I mean, most teams, ownerships, front offices, coaching staffs would die, would celebrate the success that those guys had. So even though we didn't win the title at that point, we were aware of how much success that is and how hard it is to win and get to that point, and we did not take that for granted."

It seemed that every offseason, rumors were flying about Brown being dealt; he was going to be included in a trade for Anthony Davis, maybe Jimmy Butler, or Kevin Durant. J.B. showed some sensitivity at times—nobody likes to be talked about like that—but it had to mean the world to him for J.T. to stand up for him. "I've always told him that maybe I could have done a better job of voicing my feelings in the public eye," Tatum said. "He always knew that I wanted him here. I would always tell him like, 'Man, I don't get involved with any of those talks.' I never went to Brad or went to any player like, 'Yo, I want this guy in, I want this guy out of here.' I show up and I want to do my job and play basketball. And looking back on in those moments, I didn't know how that could affect somebody because I was never in that situation. I feel like maybe I could have done a better job of publicly saying, 'No, we don't want anybody. We want J.B.'"

But behind the scenes, the dynamic duo just kept improving. "They get incrementally better each year. Those guys just keep working. I think probably the biggest thing is their supporting cast was just better. It fit better. We just have a ton of talent this year that fit very well together," Ainge said.

"They play through injuries, they play when they're tired, they play when they're sick, and they show up for these playoff games, and they show up in the big moments, and they make the game easier for their teammates. To me, that's the real leadership, just bringing it every day. And I think they've just slowly gotten better as players, but they have had that competitive integrity their whole careers with us."

Even with all the criticism—Tatum isn't clutch; Brown makes too many turnovers—you'll notice that you *never* hear anything bad about either of them as teammates or, more importantly, as humans. "One of the things that I feel really good about in this moment right now [is] I didn't think any less of Jaylen, Jayson, and everybody else that hadn't won one six days ago," Stevens told NBA TV after winning the title. "They're still the same guys. They're still the same people. They're special, they're unique, and we're just fortunate to be the last team standing."

The Boston Globe's Dan Shaughnessy was one of many in the media who harped on the fact that the Jays hadn't won a championship, going as far as to say they were entitled. Now, that's all moot. "I just felt that the years of service they had in the league, seven, eight years—that's a long time to be in the NBA. I just thought, *Yeah, they're due. They've got to do this. They've got to step up and do it.* Now they have," Shaughnessy explained. "They're in the club. That goes away forever. Just see what they can add on to it. I think it was very gratifying for the two of them. They were going to hear that until they won one. Now they have, so they don't have to hear it."

One of my good friends in broadcasting is former NBA champion Jim Chones, who now does the Cavaliers games in Cleveland. He is a really smart guy who played with Magic Johnson, Kareem Abdul-Jabbar, and others. Two years ago he told me that for the Celtics to win that they'd have to trade either Tatum or Brown—they couldn't play together. After this year he said simply, "I was wrong. They *can* play together."

Damn right they can, and I expect both of them to take even more ownership of the team moving forward. They've seen what they can do, and once you get a taste of that, you don't want to go back. In the *Time* magazine story about Brown, he summed up his relationship with Tatum best. "We have a championship-level relationship," he said. "History is going to remember us both for what we accomplished this past season, and I think we have a lot more in store for people."

CHAPTER TWENTY

K.P.

As much as Kristaps Porzingis has contributed on the court—a post presence, a shot blocker, and great three-point shooter—one of the biggest things he brought was *off* the court: joy. He was so happy to be in Boston, and that attitude has been infectious. One of the surprising gems was his relationship with Jaylen Brown. What would a white guy from Latvia have in common with a brother from Georgia? Apparently, a lot. Joe Mazzulla coined them "Cookies and Cream," a nickname that stuck throughout the season.

Brown is a serious guy, and to the outside world, he can sometimes seem aloof. He likes things the way he likes them; so, his first interaction with his new teammate was a little surprising. J.B. got on the team plane and headed to his normal seat—the one he'd been sitting in for the past four seasons. When he got there, he found a 7'2" center occupying his spot. What did Brown say? "Brother, brother, brother, that's my seat," he said. "I'm like because it's K.P., I allowed him to do it though."

The new teammates sat together and talked the entire flight, and a friendship was born.

Porzingis even ended up buying a condo in the same building as his new BFF. Jaylen has always gotten along with his teammates, but it seemed to be more like coworkers. I'd made the comment that I had never seen him and Jayson Tatum hug or get excited with each other. That changed last year.

An amazing aspect of Porzingis is his relatability, and it manifested itself on and off the court. Brown had a great year, but in the past, he's never gotten enough credit because he's a no-nonsense guy. I've never seen him smile as much as he has since K.P. joined the team. They're the oddest couple since Danny DeVito and Arnold Schwarzenegger in *Twins* in the late 1980s. It felt like Brown was releasing something. The two brothers from another mother just got into each other, and it was so cool to see. Somehow, he'd been able to drag Brown's personality out of him, which I think was one of the biggest developments of the season. You saw a relaxed, happy, enthusiastic J.B.

That chemistry played out in a big way *on* the court. "I just feel like the connection, the behind-the-back passes, the back cuts. It's like you guys know where each other are gonna be at all times," Brown said. "Our games really just complement each other, like him being a great shooter and then also a lob threat puts teams in a difficult position, especially when I'm trying to get downhill because it just makes the read easy. I mean, I could throw it up if you step up or if he pops and I'm just hitting him on a pop, and then I can just hit him every time."

K.P. said their connection off the court helps on the court. "It helps us in terms of being able to communicate with each other, say things to each other, and not take it personally because we're cool off the court also," he said. "And that way you can kind of push each other and tell each other things maybe that are not things you would say to somebody you're not as close to on the court. And I think that's where we have that advantage because of our relationship off the court."

You can probably figure out who is the cookie and who's the cream, but to take it a step further: what K.P. brings offensively is definitely best described as a warm cookie. I loved Rob Williams, and he was a huge part of what the Boston Celtics did on defense. Offensively, he was good with alley-oops, but he wasn't a threat otherwise. It's not like when Jayson Tatum or Brown got doubled, they were looking to throw it out to Williams. That just wasn't his game. With K.P. you could kick it back out, and he'd nail the three. You know how you're on an airplane, and the flight attendant brings you a cookie? That's all fine and good, but when that cookie is warm? Oh man! That's what Porzingis brought to the team. I mean, K.P. did that stuff with everyone, but it was most noticeable with Brown, and I don't think it's a coincidence that this was the best year of J.B.'s career.

* * *

Whenever you win a title, everyone, of course, is happy. The Jays had the huge monkey off of their backs, Jrue Holiday won with his second team, Joe Mazzulla proved he was a championship coach, and it goes on and on.

But other than possibly the Jays, I don't know if there was *anyone* happier than Kristaps Porzingis. My impression of him beforehand was that he was a loser; he'd only been in the playoffs twice and never out of the first round. He was brittle, always missing games. But now he was a champion.

I think back to the first time I spoke with Porzingis. It was on an early road trip. We were on the way to the arena, and I said, "Man, they can't get the smile off your face."

He looked at me and said, "I am so happy that Brad pulled the trigger for me and made that trade." He said it in that thick accent, and I'm thinking like, *Am I in a Rocky movie here?*

During the playoff series against the Cleveland Cavaliers, K.P. was definitely not going to play, as he recovered from his injury against the Miami Heat. It was a beautiful, sunny day; so, I went out to grab some lunch. There's Porzingis and his girlfriend, sitting out on the bench in front of the Ritz–Carlton like he didn't have a care in the world. One thought came to my mind: *This dude just gets it; he's on a great team, having the time of his life. Even though he's hurt, he'll come back and all will be good again.*

Austin Ainge noticed Porzingis' mood right away, too. "From the moment he got here, was just thrilled to be here and wanting to win and with a smile on his face," Ainge said. "It did not take a lot with this group. [Porzingis and Jrue Holiday] were ready. They were at the stage of their life where they had their priorities right."

Whatever the league-wide perception of Porzingis was, I don't think he really had to prove himself to his teammates. They surely knew what type of player he was. But the fans…well, that's a different deal. But Porzingis embraced it right away. In a way he's become Kevin Garnett 2.0. "It was just natural. I love playing here. Even before I came, I loved playing here on the road. When I came here, I got so much support from the fans, and I was able to connect with the fans really well," K.P. said. "My favorite part was the parade after winning it all. Nothing but gratitude for the support we have received as a team and myself individually. It's like no place else for me."

When he returned to the floor in Game One against the Dallas Mavericks, he didn't come out with the rest of the team; the organization built the drama with a camera following him down the tunnel. I thought this was just brilliant. As he approached the floor, the crowd absolutely went berserk. This was all new to him—he sure as hell didn't get this type of reception in New York when he played for the Knicks. Nor did he get it in Dallas or Washington, D.C.

I give him all the credit in the word for not only returning for Game One, but also after getting re-injured in Game Two, he talked his way back to action for Game Five. There may not be another player on this squad as happy to be a member of the Boston Celtics as K.P. This was a second lease on life for the big guy. It kind of reminded me of another injury-prone center who came to Boston to win a ring. The easy comparison is Porzingis with Bill Walton.

Of course, Walton had an incredible college career; so, everyone knew who he was when he entered the NBA. Porzingis, on the other hand, was an unknown over here, just a big guy from Latvia who looked and sounded like Ivan Drago in *Rocky IV*. Both were very good—Walton won the MVP and led the Portland Trail Blazers to a championship, while

Porzingis was an All-Star by his third year and had won over skeptical fans in New York. By the time Red Auerbach traded me for Walton, the big man had only played in 378 games in his career (out of a possible 902). When Brad Stevens went and got K.P., he had been available for 402 of his team's 656 games. They both had something to prove when they came to Boston with a key difference being that Porzingis was about five years younger.

Still, both moves were filled with risk. With the Walton trade, the team lost me, a two-time champion with a reputation of playing my best in big games. For K.P., Stevens sent away a guy considered the heart and soul of the team in Marcus Smart. Both big guys won a title in their first season in Green. *The Boston Globe*'s Bob Ryan is hoping that's where the similarities end.

"Walton was just so dramatic about it. The way he went out after having that wonderful year and he gets hurt immediately in a non-playing manner," Ryan said, comparing him to Porzingis. "He's still 28 years old…And big men do have longer careers as a rule. They're not running up and down as far as everybody else, especially now since the low post is going to hell."

CHAPTER TWENTY-ONE

TWO FOR JRUE

The fit was so perfect; it was almost like destiny. Once Damian Lillard went to the Milwaukee Bucks and Jrue Holiday to the Portland Trail Blazers, it was a race to see which Eastern Conference power could get him. Fortunately, Brad Stevens was able to snag him quickly. Before this trade the Boston Celtics had already dealt Marcus Smart for Kristaps Porzingis (and signed him to a contract extension). There was a legitimate question of whether that move was enough. "I figured before Holiday it was still: 'How much different are they from last year?' I don't know," *The Boston Globe*'s Dan Shaughnessy said. "They got Porzingis instead of Smart. That's kind of a weird thing."

Whereas there was still a question about how Porzingis would fit on a winning team, the fact that Holiday had a ring from Milwaukee was proof that he would. "We thought Jrue was a winning player, could help us win, and was an amazing player and person," Austin Ainge said. "And so we just thought it would be great to get him. But the fact that he had a ring didn't, wasn't the biggest factor. Just the person that he is was the biggest factor."

Some initially wondered how Holiday would fit in with the Jays, K.P., Derrick White, and Al Horford, but I never had a question. Holiday is pretty much a chameleon. He does whatever the team wants, whatever the team needs, on a given night. He's unlike so many great players in the league in that he doesn't need the spotlight and doesn't need the ball to be better. He defends his ass off all the time—that's a given. But there's so much more. He's like a Swiss army knife, which can do so many different things. That is Holiday in a nutshell. He comes into any situation in a very quiet but confident way and demands respect—not in a look-at-me kind of way but more of a just-do-your-job manner. He's a fun dude to be around and gets along with all his teammates so well.

As far as the Bucks went, they were the trendy pick to win the East, but I wanted to know how they were going to fit together because Lillard is a great scorer, but defense isn't his thing. There are going to be times in a game when you're going to need to tighten up the defense. How were they going to do that when they didn't have that Holiday dude? They can talk all they want about "Fear the Deer," but I didn't because I thought they had lost their heart and soul. "It's been fun. It's been fun. It's been a challenge," Holiday said. "My responsibilities here are a bit different than on the other teams were like in Milwaukee. I had to score and defend the best player almost every night, but those two constants were something that I knew I was gonna do in here."

Sure, Lillard is going to the Hall of Fame, but I don't think Milwaukee is ever going to realize what they lost in Holiday. I knew he was a really good player but didn't realize he was so efficient at scoring from the outside. And these shots will just come at odd times. Sometimes the team would struggle offensively, and then Holiday would pull up and knock down the jumper. That was definitely an eye-opener.

Even in the short time he's been on the team, he's the guy I feel closest to in terms of the job he has. I played with Larry Bird, Robert Parish, Kevin McHale, Nate Archibald, and Dennis Johnson—five Hall of Famers. By the time they came to the team, I was our leading scorer. That changed in a hurry. Bill Fitch made sure I knew my new job was to guard the opposition's top player. I could either get with the program or I wouldn't be around long. But there were times when the team needed me to score—like in Game Seven of the 1984 NBA Finals against the Los Angeles Lakers. When I sensed that need, I delivered. Holiday is the same way.

Bob Ryan, an institution at *The Boston Globe*, appreciates the no-ego approaches of Holiday and White. "You're so lucky to find people like that. It's just the ideal. And then you got two of them, two absolutely team-oriented guys that absolutely—they don't bullshit you if they want to say, 'I don't care about the score, I don't care how many points I had, I don't care how many shots I got, I just want to win and help my team win.' But these guys, you can truly believe it," Ryan said. "How many guys can you know in their heart of hearts they're not lying? No, we have two of them. I'm saying it's almost unfair, just like the rest of the league says, 'Hey, I'd like one of these guys, how did they get two?'"

Holiday can score in critical situations, make plays, and defend—and he does it all with little fanfare. He goes about playing D differently than Smart did. Holiday is very, very stoic; I don't remember hearing him say anything on the court. Smart wore his heart on his sleeve, and if you didn't hear him barking out instructions, it's because you weren't listening.

* * *

After winning his second title, Jrue Holiday recalled those first days with the Boston Celtics in an interview with NBA TV. "I just did my best to see where I fit in when I first came," he said. "I mean, Joe made it known what he expected out of me, and then from Jason to J.B. to Al to D-White, they all made it known what they expected out of me. So, it made it really easy to come in here and just kind of gel."

But what was more difficult was converting the rooting interests of his family, who grew up in Southern California. "All my family to this day still Laker fans. I got family that came to the game in Boston with Lakers stuff on. I'm like, 'You got me messed up, thinking that you gonna come and watch this game with a LeBron jersey on. What is wrong with you?'" Holiday said. "Yeah, that's crazy to me, but that's the rivalry. That's like the history behind it. But being in that Celtic green, bro, like the pressure, it's different."

As someone who's spent more than 30 years in this city, I can tell you the man is correct, and it's certainly different than playing in Milwaukee. With the Bucks he played with a nice supporting cast in Giannis Antetokounmpo, Khris Middleton, and Brook Lopez. No offense to those guys, but teaming up with the Jays was a step up in class. "It's not just me doing all of it, which is great," Holiday said. "Sharing the load is awesome, and then scoring-wise, you know J.T. and J.B. are the load of the scoring, but the playmaking is also them. Getting used to spot up threes and shots like that. So it's been an adjustment, but it's been really, really fun."

And as great as Jayson Tatum and Jaylen Brown have been on the court, they hadn't escaped the criticism—until they finally won the title. Holiday was impressed with their mental toughness. "I saw that from Day One, bro. You know J.T., and I mean, you know J.B., too, but you know J.T., like, super cool and calm. It don't seem like anything messed with him," Holiday explained on Draymond Green's podcast. "But I know just being here and seeing that type of pressure, bro, I'm like, man, I really admire it, and they do it [with such] a grace, and just how to handle themselves is wise beyond their years. So, it's been, it's been cool to kind of see that."

Holiday meshed so well on the champs. The best word to describe him is *winner*. He's not about the flash; he's about the W. Think about a guy like Ja Morant. He has so much more talent than Holiday. If you're looking for great highlights, Morant is your guy. But if you want to win, you're taking Holiday all day. That's just his mentality; it's what he lives for, stats be damned. "I would push back on that and say the sacrifice to me would be scoring 20 and winning 20 games. That would be worse, much, much worse," Austin Ainge said. "And that should be the terrible outcome, and I think that we need to reframe all of that, but still that is a reality at times, that the guys worry about shots, but this group was not hard at all. Jrue came in just wanting to win."

Brad Stevens expounded on how infectious that winning attitude is. "One of the things that we think is a really important character trait is self-awareness. Knowing who you are, knowing what you do best, and being willing to do that for the good of the team. I think that Drew is the best example of that maybe in the league," Stevens said. "Derrick White's nipping at his heels, Kristaps Porzingis is nipping at his heels. Al is another great example, right? We're loaded with guys that know who they are and do it the right way, play the right way. That's why all the talk about the individual stuff—who cares?"

And that is why the guy has two rings. Holiday is the first player in NBA history to do so in his first year with two different teams.

CHAPTER TWENTY-TWO

D-WHITE

When Derrick White came to Boston, nobody was quite sure what we'd be getting, but living under the radar is nothing new for this guy. When White graduated from high school, he didn't receive a single scholarship offer from *any* four-year college. He ended up going to Division II's Colorado-Colorado Springs in exchange for a small stipend to help with room and board. He dominated there, scoring nearly 26 points, seven rebounds, and five assists a game.

For his senior season, White transferred to the University of Colorado. He sat out a year (back when transfer rules were different) and then was named first-team All-Pac-12, scoring 18 a game and perhaps, more importantly, being named to the conference's all-defensive team. He was a surprise pick by the San Antonio Spurs near the end of the first round of the 2017 NBA Draft and played mostly in the G League his rookie season, only playing 17 games for the Spurs.

The next season he became a solid rotation player and occasional starter. Still, nobody really paid attention to him. Fortunately, one of the assistant coaches in San Antonio when White was coming up was a guy by the name of Ime Udoka. His familiarity with White certainly influenced Brad Stevens to make the trade to get him as did a set of exhibition games. "It was back in 2019, and he was a young kid on the U.S.

select team, and they were playing the Olympians," Brad Stevens said. "I just love the way he competed and played, and it just felt like he always made the right basketball play."

Right away, it just seemed like D-White was meant to be here. His first few games, he was obviously trying to get his footing. I was thinking, *That man has a pretty good shot, but they're not going in.* Eventually, they started to fall. Then he became this playmaker who could score, rebound, and, of course, play defense. Whether he was guarding the other team's point guard or shooting guard, nothing fazed him.

In that half-season after coming to the Boston Celtics, White was inconsistent. Even though the Celtics lost to the Golden State Warriors in the NBA Finals, I think there was one play that was his signature moment. Steph Curry pinned him on the three-point line. White had lost his dribble. So, he tried faking, then just launched this long three, and it went in. Curry just shook his head in disbelief. It felt like White was saying, "Okay, I'm here, and I'm legit. I can do this." This was a real welcome-to-Boston moment.

The city can be a tough place to play if you're a low-key dude. I think White has a real downshift personality. He ain't Marcus Smart, that's for sure. You know I love Smart, but he's in your grill 24/7. You're either going to love him or hate him. With White it's just all good. He never says anything, never gets in anyone's face. He just hits his shot and runs back on defense. He almost never says anything to the officials, but when he does, it actually means something. When he tells Joe Mazzulla to challenge a call, Coach will do it without even checking with his assistants. Compare that to when Al

Horford or one of the Jays does it; Mazzulla *always* looks with his other coaches for confirmation then.

It can be difficult for a quiet guy like D-White to fit in on a superstar-laden team like the Celtics. Not that I'm quiet, but I think about my role on a roster that had four Hall of Famers on it. The first year that Larry Bird came to us, Bill Fitch pulled me aside and told me my role was changing; my new assignment was to guard the best player on the other team. In my head I was like, *Yo, I just scored 19 points a game. Now you want to make me a defensive specialist?* But it obviously worked, and we won two championships.

White put whatever ego he had aside and left it at the front door. That's what you have to do in order to win. But here's the thing—when you do that and you win, you see your reward. If you come up short, you don't see that reward, and it becomes a conflict. But since coming here White has won the title, received a contract extension, and won a gold medal in the Olympics. Despite those lofty accomplishments, I don't worry about it going to his head.

When I was in San Antonio, I was hanging out near the River Walk. I saw a taco stand—nothing fancy—and decided to grab a bite. The players have all their meals catered; they eat in fancy restaurants. But as I went to get my taco, who's there? White. He just said, "Hey," grabbed his taco, and headed out. No entourage, no nothing.

Everyone remembers great plays from the championship run, and White made plenty of them, but the image he'll most be remembered for came just before halftime of Game Five. The Celtics were in control, up by 12 points, when

D-White dove for a loose ball…and had Dallas Mavericks center Dereck Lively fall right on his head, smashing his face to the floor. Just for perspective: Lively is seven feet tall and weighs 216 pounds. White is 6'4", 190. D-White lost that battle—and a good part of his front tooth. ABC/ESPN had Jaylen Brown mic'd up. He said, "Boy, you sure is ugly!" That was a hilarious memory for everyone. Before reporting to 2024 training camp, White had just undergone his *third* root canal. But as D-White said after Game Five, "I'd lose all my teeth for a championship."

It's that attitude that makes White the perfect Celtic on and off the court. "You'll hear superlatives attached to players like great teammate, hard worker, unselfish, never has a bad day, all those things," Stevens said. "And most of the times, I would say if people are saying that, it's somewhat true. With Derrick it's all true every day. And his spirit, his teamness, his competitiveness, and yet perspective on life, he just makes you smile."

Even when he's missing a few teeth, apparently.

The summer of 2024 might be known as the summer of D-White. He won the championship and signed a four-year contract extension worth $125 million. "It was amazing. I've been saying that since I've been here that I didn't want to go nowhere else, and I just love playing for this organization, with this team, this coaching staff, and for these fans," he said. "So I was super excited for it to get done, especially early in the summer. So I didn't have to answer all the questions about it, but, yeah, I love being here, and me and my family are super excited to be here for a while."

Then came the biggest surprise—a trip to Paris to play on Team USA. "I'm just getting that phone call. I was just kind of at home chilling, relaxing. And just getting the call and just being a part of that team with legends of the game, people that are the best in this game that the game has right now," White said, "I just think when you're around great players every day for about a month and a half, you got no choice but to pick up what makes them great, what makes them special—from what they eat, from like the preparation, how they take care of their bodies, what they do in the weight room, so just all those little things off the court, which you don't really get to see unless you're on their team. So, I think that was probably the coolest part for me and then just like on the court just and how they compete, just how they're focused on all the little things. And it was just really cool to see the day-in-and-day-out process of legends of this game."

Not bad for a guy who couldn't get a scholarship out of high school.

* * *

Over the years the Boston Celtics have had some terrific backcourts. Obviously, Bob Cousy and Sam Jones are both in the Hall of Fame for a reason. Cooz was the ballhandling wizard, and Jones' jumper was smooth as silk. Throw in K.C. Jones' defense, and the Celtics were unbeatable.

When I played we had Tiny Archibald and Chris "Doc" Ford. Tiny was ahead of his time in terms of playmaking and scoring. Doc was so smart and a terrific shooter who hit the first three-pointer in NBA history. The 1984 team had two of my great friends, Danny Ainge and Dennis Johnson. Ainge could shoot from anywhere and saw the game so well. D.J. was just a championship player. His stats never jumped out at you, but with the game on the line, he's the guy you wanted out there. Larry Bird said D.J. was the best player he ever shared the court with.

The 2024 champs had a unique starting backcourt with Jrue Holiday and Derrick White.

I can tell you I've never seen a better defensive backcourt; I mean, these guys are shot blockers, they make steals, they've been finishing themselves, they make passes. They're extraordinary. *The Boston Globe*'s Bob Ryan said it's like Holiday and White have PhDs in basketball. "They're all around, they do everything. They play offense, defense, they make the right play," he explained. "The thing about it that is interesting is that I think most teams in the league would—at any time in history—would be happy to have one of these guys, that type of player."

Ryan also cites the backcourt of Jo Jo White and John Havlicek (both Hall of Famers) as a dynamic duo, but he said the way that Holiday and D-White mesh together skill-wise and team-wise sets them apart. "They are so just perfectly suited for the task," he said. "I've never seen a pairing quite like that."

Holiday has averaged 21 points a night, been an All-Star, and made a ton of money. But I'm sure if you asked him for his biggest accomplishments, they would be team-oriented: winning two NBA titles and two Olympic golds. White is four years younger than his backcourt mate and has always been a background player if you will, never making an All-Star team. But like Holiday, he's an outstanding defender and can be a scorer, playmaker, or anything else the team needs. You think about what they've done, winning games and playing off Jayson Tatum and Brown, and I just kind of smile when I think about them as players and seeing their growth. When you have two great players with that mind-set, it's tough to beat.

CHAPTER TWENTY-THREE

THE HALF-COURT MASTER AND SAMMY THE SHOOTER

There's a third member of the Boston Celtics backcourt who's become invaluable: Payton Pritchard. In any championship series, there are signature moments. Obviously, Kristaps Porzingis coming back from injury in Game One of the Finals was incredible, the stuff legends are made of. But there were two shots that Celtics fans will never forget. They weren't game-winning buzzer-beaters, but they were incredible.

In Game Two time was winding down in the third quarter. The Celtics led by six when Jayson Tatum threw the inbounds pass to Pritchard with only 3.3 seconds left. Pritchard caught it at his own free-throw line and raced down the floor. He took a step past halfcourt and let it fly. The ball was on line, banked off the backboard, and went in! Talk about taking the heart out of your opponent. In the deciding Game Five, he did it again! Just before halftime he let it go again beyond halfcourt and swished it.

I've won titles in the Boston Garden and been in there for some really special moments. But I've *never* heard the crowd any louder than after that particular shot. If the Dallas Mavericks had any thoughts about trying to come back, they ended right then and there. It's funny. I'll go on YouTube and see the superfans who hate the Celtics. They watch Pritchard hit that shot, and they're like, "Who the fuck is this guy coming in and taking this shot? He did it again? Jesus Christ!" I love it.

The box score will show that he only played 62 minutes over five games in the Finals—and only 1:25 in the clincher—but Mr. Pritchard definitely left his mark.

Obviously, nobody expects anyone to make those shots, but Pritchard has overcome the odds his entire career. When the Celtics took him with the 26th pick in 2020, it didn't make sense. Kemba Walker was still here, as was Marcus Smart. The team didn't need a point guard, but you can never have too much toughness. "My dad would lovingly call him a 'psycho.' A basketball psycho is a positive thing. And he is," Austin Ainge said. "He's so intense and so competitive. We just knew that Payton just wouldn't let himself fail. He was going to fight and work until he found his way to help to get on the court."

At 6'1" with short arms, Pritchard doesn't really look like an NBA player, but this guy's bite is much worse than his bark. Teams try to post him up with bigger guards, but Pritchard doesn't give an inch. When you have young superstars who are getting paid, it's so important to be able to fill out the roster with good role players. Pritchard is one of those nickel-and-dime guys, even though he makes close to $7 million. (That is nickels and dimes these days.) But he is a true gym rat. I remember Tatum telling me that every single day, "Pritchard is the guy who, at the end of practice, wants to go one-on-one." P.P. is like the gum on the bottom of your doggone shoe.

Offensively, he can obviously shoot the ball. This cat scored 92 points in a Portland Pro-Am game a few years ago. I know it doesn't count, but 92 points is 92 points. But because he was stuck behind Marcus Smart, Malcolm Brogdon, and Derrick White, Pritchard only played in 48 games in 2023, and that led to him asking for a trade. The team knew the request was simply a result of his fire burning up to the surface. "Yeah, he was frustrated at times with us not playing. The guy just wants to play, and we knew that about Payton," Ainge said. "We knew he liked our guys, and it wasn't ever a personal thing. He just really wants to play. It's his life. It's his everything. We felt bad for him because we knew he was a good player and could play on a lot of teams. We just didn't always have the right spots for him, and it would go up and down. It's just a credit to his toughness and drive to just stay ready and keep getting better and keep waiting for chances to prove to the stars on the team and the coaches and the rest of the league that he can really play and deserves the minutes."

Jaylen Brown puts it simply: "Payton is a killer, and he's always looking to put pressure on a defense. If you don't put pressure on him and you don't guard him, he'll light you up."

When asked for comparisons to Pritchard, Bob Ryan, longtime writer for *The Boston Globe*, goes way back in time to a combination of Larry Siegfried (from the 1960s) and either Jerry Sichting of the 1986 team or Eddie House from 2008. "He's the same size roughly, maybe a little bit taller than Siegfried, but he's tough and feisty and aggressive, scrappy. And I also say he's good for at least one sneaky offensive rebound a game," Ryan said. "Jerry was a foul-line and 17-foot shooter but not remotely a three-point shooter, and, of course, Pritchard is a great, outstanding three-point shooter. But

Eddie House was a three-point shooter, too. But I do think it's just in terms of providing offense off the bench and then providing that scrappiness that was Siegfried's hallmark, he's a combination of those two."

Even during the championship run, Pritchard's playing time was inconsistent, but he made his presence felt whenever he was on the court. He is one of my favorites. He's a little confident…make that a lot confident and a lot arrogant. Having pieces like him, Sam Hauser, Luke Kornet to come in and understand their roles is essential.

And Pritchard has come a long way. "A lot of us have to start from the ground up," he said. "We're not going to be high draft picks. So, you have to get it through your work, showing up every day, grinding; so, that's how I've gotten to this point now. Come in, do the little things, you never know how far you can take it."

This guy took it all the way to a championship ring—and two unforgettable shots in the Finals. "Payton Pritchard, like unreal, right?" Jaylen Brown said. "Like just comes in the game and drains one from halfcourt. That dude, he's a fucking legend, man. Shout out to Payton Pritchard."

* * *

As really good teams evolve, they kind of get hamstrung when it comes to finances. Think about how the Golden State Warriors got into their financial bind because they drafted Steph Curry, Klay Thompson, and Draymond Green. They obviously all turned into future Hall of Famers. So, their salaries got crazy. As a result, they paid a massive luxury tax, and with the new restrictions in the collective bargaining agreement, they would be facing severe penalties.

With Jayson Tatum and Jaylen Brown both getting super-max contracts—and eventually paying Kristaps Porzingis, Al Horford, and Jrue Holiday—Boston Celtics management has to find quality guys who don't make a ton of money to fill out the roster. Nobody is a better example of this than Sam Hauser.

Hauser was a solid—not great—college player, spending three years at Marquette and then transferring to Virginia. He was good for around 15 points a game. Somewhat surprisingly on draft night, Hauser didn't hear his name called. In the second round that year, there weren't a lot of guys who have had successful careers. Clearly, Hauser should have been selected by someone.

The Celtics didn't have a first rounder, having traded it to the Oklahoma City Thunder to bring Horford back. So they'd have to be creative to add someone to their bench. Fortunately, the team had compiled a list of guys who might be available. Management wasn't surprised that he had gone undrafted. "We were not that surprised on draft night, but obviously us and the whole league were wrong. I mean, Sam should have gone in the first round as good of a player as he is," Austin Ainge said. "And part of that is the league not evaluating him correctly, and part of that is Sam getting better. And where to draw that line is hard to do even in hindsight, but Sam has turned himself into a very, very good player."

Assistant general manager Dave Lewin told *The Boston Globe* that there was plenty to like about Hauser. "Brad immediately took a liking to Sam," Lewin said. "He was impressed with his size, he was impressed with his shooting, he was impressed with his feel for the game."

One of the teams that expressed interest in Sam was the Miami Heat, who have a deep history of strong player development. "I saw what Duncan [Robinson] had done and Max Strus had done [with the Heat]," Hauser told *The Globe*. "Obviously, they have a good culture for producing guys like that."

But Celtics management zoned in on its target and pounced, offering him a two-way contract, which would allow him to be active for up to 50 NBA games. Boston sold him on its vision of him being a contributor. "We actually had a guy that's not just going to be hanging onto the end of our roster to make some shots in garbage time," Lewin said. "He was a guy we needed to get on the court because he could really play."

During his first season with the Celtics, Hauser shuttled back and forth to Maine to play with our G League team. He got into 26 games in Boston, not really making much of a mark. He only scored double figures twice. The real work, though, was being done in Portland, Maine, where Ainge said Hauser was learning what it takes to go from being a player to becoming a weapon. "He showed us that he's way better defensively than we thought and that he worked very hard to add to his shooting versatility, which means more than just catch and shoot, like moving, cutting, finding ways to get more shots off," Ainge said. "Those were the things that we saw him get better at and that we noticed more from him that gave us confidence."

That development started to show in year two. Hauser saw action in 80 games, even getting eight starts. He averaged six-and-a-half points in roughly 16 minutes a night. The process was coming along. One important thing that Hauser learned was how to adapt defensively. Listen: he's never going to be Jrue Holiday, but guys used to pick on him relentlessly like they do with Duncan Robinson. Hauser knows he's not the best defender, but he learned how to compensate. He does a terrific job of studying his opponents. So, he is aware of where they want to get the ball. He's not going to beat them to their spot with his feet. Instead he knows the angles and tendencies and beat them there with his mind. Because of film study, he's learned how to anticipate where the ball is going and he comes up with his share of steals.

He's different than I was as a young player. That's for sure. I remember my first time going against Dr. J. I just stood there, thinking, *Wow, that's a nice move! Oooh, that is, too,* as he lit my ass up repeatedly.

Hauser's shot is always going to be his calling card, but by giving some effort on the other end of the floor, he's earned his spot in the rotation. In the championship season, Hauser was a bona fide contributor; averaging nine points a game, even dropping 10 three-pointers against the Washington Wizards.

Then came the playoffs, and it was the first time the team really counted on Hauser during the postseason, and his play started off with a bang. Against the Heat and Cleveland Cavaliers, Hauser was on fire, shooting nearly 50 percent from downtown. But in the Eastern Conference Finals, Hauser hit the skids, only making two of his 16 long-ball attempts. For a guy known as a shooter, this could have wrecked his confidence.

Hauser may have come into the league as sort of a one-trick pony, but Joe Mazzulla's trust in him never waned. Ainge says the threat of what he could do was still valuable. "Even if he's not making every shot in the game, teams are still terrified of him," Ainge said. "They know that he's just a deadly, deadly shooter. And so even when...he goes 0–3 in a game...the guys have to stay with him. The opposing teams know he's one of the best shooters in the world. And then his defense is solid, and he never makes mistakes."

Empowered by his team's belief in him, Hauser returned to form against the Dallas Mavericks. Hauser was back to normal, making 11 of his 23 three-pointers and helping us win the title. He tried to explain his mind-set: "In the moment you're so locked in on the game that you're not really thinking about it."

But afterward? "You just kind of reflect on the game, like *Whoa, I just made a couple of shots in the NBA Finals.* That's pretty cool."

That's pretty good for a guy who never heard his name called on draft night.

CHAPTER TWENTY-FOUR

BIG AL

When guys say they're trying to win a championship for a specific person, sometimes they mean it; sometimes they do not. But I can tell you there isn't a player on the Boston Celtics who didn't want to get that ring for Al Horford. His journey to a title was not easy.

At the University of Florida, Horford was the glue on a team that featured NBA players Joakim Noah and Corey Brewer. His coach was Billy Donovan, and the Gators won consecutive NCAA championships. His coach knew what he had in Horford, even though he was only 20. "He has got an unbelievable ability to impact winning and impact the locker room. The one thing that everyone would say about him is that as a teammate he's phenomenal, and there's no intention by him other than to win," said Donovan, who noted what Horford brought off the court was just as valuable. "He has a great pulse. He can tell you what's going on with every guy inside the team…He was great with me. He'd say 'You need to talk with this guy a little more.' And I would imagine he's created that type of culture in Boston. There's a reason they brought him back. He's a special guy, totally about winning."

After nine years (and four All-Star appearances) with the Atlanta Hawks, he became the first major free agent to sign with the Celtics. Horford remembers Danny Ainge's sales pitch. "Man, I never forget what Danny told me. He said, 'You can win championships in many places, but there's nothing like winning in Boston, nothing like winning as a Celtic,'" Horford said. "And that stuck with me."

There was also a tangible incentive to seal the deal. "It was crazy because during free agency meetings in 2016, my agent and I, we were both sitting in the meeting, and we just kept looking at this enormous ring in Wyc's [Grousbeck] hand," Horford said. "And we both after the meeting were like, 'Did you notice that?'"

You *know* the big man wanted one of those for himself.

* * *

Al Horford changed his game with the times. After never taking more than 36 three-pointers in his first eight seasons, the number jumped to 256 for his last year with the Atlanta Hawks. In his time with the Boston Celtics, he's averaged well more than 200 attempts a season. He was never what you'd call a huge scorer, and his points per game have dropped to single digits the last couple of years, but his ability to be the adult in the room can't be measured.

Jrue Holiday, of course, had already won a championship in Milwaukee. Like Horford, he's known as an awesome guy to have on the roster. He's won the Twyman-Stokes Teammate of the Year award *three* times as well as the Joe Dumars Trophy for sportsmanship. He was desperate for his older friend to have that experience. "Once I became his teammate, it was like one of the ultimate goals of this season," Holiday said. "Knowing the type of person that Al is, knowing the leader that he is—even off the court—the father that he is, just the all-around great person and great human, I'd run through a brick wall for him. I'm so happy that he got one."

Horford is definitely a lead-by-example guy. He never says much, but when he does, people listen. I remember a game where we were broadcasting near the Celtics' bench, and out of nowhere, Horford yelled at his teammates, "Dammit, let's play hard!" I was like, *Whoa, who is that in Horford's body?* It was just shocking to see that.

The thing about Horford is that he just does his work. Really, in all my years of covering his games, the only signature moment that comes to mind was when he went at Giannis Antetokounmpo in that playoff game vs. the Milwaukee Bucks. Much like Holiday, Horford is the guy who goes into Ben & Jerry's—with like 50 different flavors—and orders chocolate. Not Chunky Monkey or Cherry Garcia, just chocolate.

On the court, Horford was already a four-time All-Star when he came to Boston; so, he had the street cred that was perfect for a young team. "The poise, the veteran stability, the big brother nature, he can help you in different ways," said Bob Ryan, the respected sportswriter for *The Boston Globe.* "He's made himself into a reliable three-point shooter, blocks some great blocks…He brought a lot of needed technical and emotional stability to the team."

Think about how young Jaylen Brown and Jayson Tatum still are. Now imagine what it's like going to all of those conference finals, making All-Star teams, etc. The Jays were fortunate to have Horford there to show them the way. It's telling that after winning the championship there were the two Jays, talking about Big Al. First, it was Tatum, talking about how important it was to get Horford his ring. "He don't have much time left, I hear," he said. "That's my favorite teammate of all time. He paved the way for a lot of us. It means the world to us."

Then the NBA Finals MVP weighed in. "He's been a great not just leader on the court but off the court as well, just a mentor, somebody I know I can talk to about life and is going to give me great advice about family, about finances, about just life, adversity, whatever the case is," Brown said. "Al has just been that guy for me and for us." J.B. isn't a guy who just throws around things he doesn't mean. That came from the heart.

As the championship trophy made its rounds during the offseason, Horford brought it to the Dominican Republic, where he's the first native to win an NBA title. Alongside was his coach, who reflected on the impact his center has had. "His goal in life is to just sustain success on and off the court," Joe Mazzulla said. "For him to invite me back to his hometown and watch the impact that he has on the environment but also the impact that people have on him, it was just great to see that relationship, and it was great to share that with his family and really the environment. So I was grateful that I got to go."

Brown said it simply, "It's been an honor to be by his side. And Al Horford is a real-life legend and hero. It's been great to be his teammate."

* * *

Every great team needs to have a character. Of course, they need to have character as a whole, but there has to be someone to keep the mood light. During the first half of the 1980s, yours truly filled that role with the Boston Celtics, but we were also fortunate to have guys like M.L. Carr and Kevin McHale. We did a lot of winning and had a lot of fun.

The Jays don't really have that type of personality, and neither do Jrue Holiday, Derrick White, Kristaps Porzingis, or Al Horford. That is why Luke Kornet is so important. He grew up around the game, as his dad, Frank, spent a couple of seasons with the Milwaukee Bucks. Like his father, Luke went to Vanderbilt—not exactly a basketball powerhouse— where he didn't even average double figures until his senior season. But with his 7'2" frame and tireless work ethic, he's cobbled together an NBA career with the New York Knicks, Chicago Bulls, Cleveland Cavaliers, Bucks, and Celtics. This is his second stint in Boston.

Prior to the last two seasons in green, Kornet had never played in more than 46 games in a single year. But he's definitely found his niche on this team. When the roster is fully healthy, he knows he's not going to play a ton, but he also knows that Horford hasn't played both ends of back-to-back games in a while, and with both Rob Williams two years ago and Porzingis now, the other big men have been injury prone.

Kornet's not going to make an All-Star team, but he serves a purpose on the floor, getting rebounds, blocking shots, and playing physical defense. When he came into the league, he took three-to-four three-pointers a game. But in the championship season, he took just one. (But he made it; so, he shot 100 percent.)

The guys love themselves some Kornet, and it's easy to see why. When we played in Indiana last season, he went to the line for a couple of big free throws against the Pacers. He made them both—then made a gesture like he was sticking a needle in his arm to show that he had ice water in his veins! Who does that? That's vintage Celtics stuff from the 1980s right there.

You'll never hear a peep from Kornet about playing. He's grateful for whatever minutes he gets and he'll bust his ass every single night. Maybe he wouldn't fit in on some other teams, but for this group of guys, he's perfect. When he makes a big hoop or blocks a shot, the bench just loses it. They're legitimately happy just like he is when they do something. Guys like him and Sam Hauser are the glue that keeps everything together.

* * *

Obviously, the Boston Celtics didn't need much at the 2024 trading deadline. They already were stacked beyond belief, and everyone was relatively healthy. Xavier Tillman, who reached the Final Four for Tom Izzo at Michigan State after defeating Zion Williamson's Duke team, wasn't a superstar, but he'd been a good rotation piece for the Memphis Grizzlies the past couple of years. At 6'8", 245 pounds, he was a bruising big, playing about 20 minutes a night, chipping in six or seven points and around five rebounds for the

Grizzlies. His main job was to use his size, and he did it well. The previous couple of years, Memphis finished as the second seed in the loaded Western Conference.

Brad Stevens decided you can never have enough size and traded Lamar Stevens and two second-round picks for X. Right away, X and I had a connection. I hadn't ever spoken to him, but he came up to me one day and told me his stepfather was a huge fan of mine and asked if I'd take a picture with him. It was pretty funny because I'm sure he had no idea who I was, but it was all good.

Tillman wasn't a star, but he was a guy who Joe Mazzulla learned how to use in an effective way. Being a bench player isn't easy. Guys like Jayson Tatum, Jaylen Brown, and the rest of the starters all played at least 30 minutes a game, and even ol' Al Horford wasn't too far off that pace. Those guys would get a chance to feel their way into a rhythm. But for the bench squad, they might get three or four minutes at a time, and then they're out. So, they better make that time count.

After Kristaps Porzingis was injured in Game Two of the Finals, X got his opportunity in Game Three. The numbers only show that he played 11 minutes, hit a three, and had four rebounds, but with Luke Kornet out due to a wrist injury, those 11 minutes were important, and the Celtics outscored the Dallas Mavericks by nine while he was on the floor.

CHAPTER TWENTY-FIVE

BRAD STEVENS

When you see how most of Brad Stevens' moves have worked out, you can see that he was born for this job—even if none of us anticipated it. Think about it. Since he's been team president, the team has reacquired Al Horford; traded for Derrick White, Kristaps Porzingis, and Jrue Holiday; signed Luke Kornet and Sam Hauser; and won a title. For a guy who was considered a lifelong coach, it's crazy stuff.

The team has taken notice. "Brad was one of the people that was able to transition from being a coach and doing something that was a little bit more day to day to being in a front office. And he was probably one of the more natural transitions we probably ever witnessed," Jaylen Brown said. "Part of that is because he went directly into that transition. And we were so close [to winning a title] that he knew exactly the pieces that we needed and were looking for. Shoutout to Brad, his transition, and his growth as a leader in the front office. And he's still young, he's still learning."

And the fact that he's still learning is a scary proposition for the rest of the league. His plan came into focus after the Boston Celtics lost to the Miami Heat in 2023. "Brad subbed out four of the top eight and got better. I doubt that's ever happened before. You're in the Final Four and you sub out four of your top eight and you get better?" Dan Shaughnessy said. "Obviously, the subtraction of Smart and then bringing in Porzingis, bringing in Holiday, it just worked magically. More adults in the room and put them across. I think that for the two Jays, this was their time."

If you talk to Stevens for five minutes, you're instantly struck by his humility. Even after having all of his moves pay off with championship No. 18, he understands how thin the line is between being the best and not quite being good enough. "You don't sit there and make a move and say, 'Okay, now we're going to win a championship.' You just know how hard it is. I mean, we've been on the precipice of it and on the doorstep of it, but a lot of things had to go our way to win in other years in advance," he said. "And some things didn't go our way, but that's just part of it. And there's a lot that goes into it."

Joe Mazzulla said Stevens' practicality was critical in finally breaking through. "I would say just his consistency," the head coach said. "If you look at him, the same things that made him a great coach make him a great GM—his ability to eliminate emotion, make great decisions based on logic, build relationships, his ability to eliminate emotion, make great decisions based on logic, build relationships with people, and communicate to have alignment."

One of the oldest adages in sports is that great players usually are not great coaches; they did things a certain way and hold their players to that same standard. I know when I briefly got into coaching, I *hated* it. So when a guy like Stevens—one of the best coaches in the NBA—is then hiring the coach, I wondered how he felt watching them making decisions that might be different than what he would do. "There's all kinds of different strategies," Stevens said. "There's all kinds of different tactics. But the bottom line is you have this team that is in a lot of ways a mold of clay. Your job as a coach is to try to mold it into the best version of itself that it can possibly be…I have never been worried about Ime or Joe doing it the way that I would have done it. I've been more worried about us getting to the end result…I think we're 99.999 percent would probably do the same things, but they're the coach, and they have the opportunity to make those calls, and I want to be very respectful of that position and how hard it is."

What does Stevens think of all this praise he has received? "I'm a genius," he deadpanned with NBC Sports Boston after Game Five of the NBA Finals. "That might be the dumbest thing ever said."

Stevens is always a guy to deflect credit, and in the same interview, he mocked his role in the team's title run. "When I say I didn't do anything, I didn't do *anything*," he said. "I sat and watched and ate popcorn in the suite for like a hundred games." He did a hell of a lot more than that.

If you know Stevens, you realize that the celebration of winning a championship is short-lived. He talks a lot about wanting to be "in the mix" and having a chance to win every year. Obviously, that doesn't mean it will end in a championship, but that's the goal. He took in the moment, and then it was time to get back to work. "I've always wondered how—if it would feel any different as far as like how you live your life, and it absolutely doesn't. It really has no bearing on what happened the next day or the day after or the day after. You just move on, and you do the next thing," Stevens said before reflecting on his college days. "With those Butler teams, if you would have told any of us before either of those seasons started that we were going to be in a Final Four in a championship game, I mean, you take it in a heartbeat, right? And 10 years later, it's just another two times you came close. So, I don't think that that's our perspective. Our perspective is just do it as well as you can. The other team's out there, too."

CHAPTER TWENTY-SIX

JOE MAZZULLA

In Joe Mazzulla's first season behind the bench, everyone had complaints about him and his unorthodox ways. He never called timeouts, was overreliant on three-point shooting, had bad substitution patterns, and everything else. Sure, he had flaws—everyone does. But remember what he walked into: he took over just days before training camp for a coach who was gone because of mysterious circumstances, and Mazzulla had no NBA head coaching experience. Oh, and he was taking over a team that had been to the Finals the previous year. He didn't get to pick his assistants, didn't get to implement most of his system. He was just trying not to crash the car.

Talk about on-the-job training.

Given all that, it's hard to say Mazzulla didn't do a good job, but the difference between that season and his second year is like night and day. A big part of that was the support Brad Stevens provided. He doesn't get enough credit, but Sam Cassell was worth his weight in gold. You're talking about a guy who did what the Boston Celtics are now trying to accomplish—winning back-to-back championships. Cassell was a hot-shot younger player with the Houston Rockets and then came to Boston to win another ring in 2008.

Another huge voice in the room was one every basketball fan heard for more than 15 years on TV—Jeff Van Gundy.

Stevens and Mazzulla hired Van Gundy as a senior consultant. Van Gundy was an NBA head coach for 11 seasons; so, he'd seen just about everything. The team never went into detail about what he did for them, but having a couple of older guys' brains to pick was certainly helpful for Mazzulla.

If there was ever a question that Mazzulla is one of one, just ask his wife, Camai. A lot of wives are subdued when it comes to the game; they want to support their husband, but they do it quietly. Not Camai. They met while they were both coaching at Glenville State University. Camai was a dual athlete there in volleyball and track and field. Much like her husband, you don't mess with Mrs. Mazzulla. While she was getting her master's degree, she worked as a court clerk and a probation officer.

When I met her, she told me that when they're home, just chilling out, they spend a lot of time talking about basketball plays. The one thing everyone tells athletes is don't bring the job home. That's not the case for Mazzulla; he's always on. Even when he goes to Boston Red Sox games, he's thinking about basketball. Stevens recalls a conversation he had with Jaylen Brown. "Jaylen said, 'Joe's going to take something from this, and we're gonna be playing shortstop or something next year to get ready for a game.' But that's just the way he thinks. I love it," Stevens said. "His brain is wired. It's always on. He isn't afraid to try things. He isn't afraid to take a day and not do only basketball-related things to make sure that maybe he hits a chord with people on things that can help resonate for the whole team."

One of the misconceptions about Mazzulla is that he's arrogant or full of himself. He's very confident in his beliefs, but that's a trait to be admired, not criticized. On JJ Redick's *The Old Man & the Three* podcast, Mazzulla talked about his authenticity when he first got the job.

"I was a behind-the-bench coach, I'm an intern. I don't have any experience being a head coach. But what I do know is I've built great relationships. I think I've built relatively good relationships with each person in this room. I know who you are as people, I know who you are as players, and I know what type of character you have. And so, I'm going to rely on that more than anything else," Mazzulla said. "I mean, they're really good at what they do. They play the game at a really, really high level. And at that time, I wasn't really good at being a head coach in the NBA because I had never done it. So why would I go in with the expectation of we're going to do it this way? And we didn't necessarily. We worked together, but 95 percent came from the character of our locker room, the guys that have been here a long time, the new guys that joined. That's kind of what I leaned on."

Given some of his dealings with the media, I think a lot of people would be shocked to hear him say that, but that's my guy. I, though, had very little idea who Mazzulla was before he got the head job. He was a guy who didn't talk much, and when he does, it's really only to people he was assigned to work with. To go from that to being *the* man of the Celtics, well—as Mazzulla told Redick—that took a lot of self-awareness. "I was going to have to let myself go emotionally. I was going to have to put myself—there's a difference between being vulnerable with a locker room full of guys that you're working with and then being vulnerable with an entire organization and being vulnerable with the world. And I wasn't ready for that part yet, and that was hard," he said. "I struggled more with the postgame. And what I learned is because if I let somebody down, that bothers me. And so if I make a decision by my standards, that I feel like I let one of my players down or I let the team down, I can't sleep at night. And so I had to get past the fact that every decision you make as a coach is not going to be perfect. You can study the film all you want. You can memorize scouting reports, you can build your substitution pattern, you can have your play call frequency by quarter, you can have all this crap figured out, and at the end of the day, I'm a human…and it's like I had to be able to live with the philosophy that every decision I make it's just not going to go well all the time." An NBA coach who realizes he doesn't have all the answers—who would have thunk it?

One of the interesting dynamics between Mazzulla and the guys is that he's not that far removed from their ages. Heck, he's two years younger than Al Horford! The fact that he is sort of from the same generation certainly helps in relating to the players. "It looks to me like he's got the room, and that's what's really important in that league," said *The Boston Globe*'s Dan Shaughnessy. "You've got to have Tatum and Brown obviously. So, that's really important. No coach today is going to call out his young players. That's not a good career move. He's on board with everybody there. He's still young…He's practicing with them. It's a whole other thing."

I can definitely attest to Mazzulla practicing with the guys. He's like 6'2", but he doesn't care. He'll throw people down. It's like he's playing street ball, and he is the chief instigator. Mazzulla's very into jiu-jitsu. So, you know he's not fucking around.

The Boston Globe's Bob Ryan has seen every Celtics coach from Tommy Heinsohn all the way to Mazzulla, and he points out one area that Mazzulla has grown since his first year. "It's the timeout thing. Now, we know there are coaches that believe that you don't overreact and panic at certain times when things aren't going well, and you want them to play their way out of it kind of thing. And I understand that and on occasion I understand that," Ryan said. "But he stubbornly went against all the norms in the beginning about when to call a timeout and when it was obvious that timeout was needed just to, 'Let's talk this over, guys. Let's stop this momentum here.' And he's now back much more conventionally. And I think that's good."

Ryan's colleague, Dan Shaughnessy, said there's one personality trait of Mazzulla's that sticks out. "He's very stubborn. I mean, really, it's amusing how stubborn he is. And there's a lot of he won't agree with you that today's Wednesday," Shaughnessy said. "He has a fairly high opinion of himself and of his abilities, and that's good. I think he goes out of his way to remind everybody that we don't know anything. I understand that. He's right, but it's unusual coming from a young guy like that. I admire him. I think he's really interesting to me. I like writing about him."

And as anyone who follows sports knows, Boston is certainly not the easiest place for players (or coaches) to have to grow up in. Managing the media and fanbase is a whole other part of the job. "I understand why it wouldn't be for everybody, but it's also if it goes well here and you earned everybody's love," Shaughnessy said, "you're enlarged beyond how great you are as well, and it never goes away. So, it works both ways. For a guy like Joe with that stubbornness and that kind of chip on his shoulder, it's going to be even tougher. I mean, here's a guy who's literally grown up as a head coach. And based on that criticism last year, I mean, it says something about him, I guess, that he's doing great."

Mazzulla has core beliefs, and those aren't going to change for the confident leader. "My security has never really been in a job or has never been in a circumstance," he said. "I mean, my security has—for my adult life—has been in my faith, has been in my relationship with my wife and my kids. And so when I got the job, it was really kind of a win/win. It was an opportunity for me to go after something, a great organization, a great team, a great locker room, great tradition. And I felt like by them giving me the job, they bet on me, who I am as a person. And it was kind of a win/win. Either I'm gonna be myself or this is gonna work or I'm gonna be myself and I'm gonna do everything I can, and it's not. So I just felt like I wasn't going to jeopardize my security and who I was for something that needed to be done as an entire team and a togetherness."

I love that Mazzulla isn't afraid to go against the grain. Jrue Holiday's first experience with his new coach was in the middle of Mazzulla's rookie season when he coached the Eastern Conference All-Stars. "I really got to talk to him and really get to know him on a personal level outside of basketball, and that was pretty cool to experience," Holiday said. "The basketball side, he does do things a little different.

I mean, Brad knows. The way that we practice and the things that we do, the attention to detail I've never experienced before, but he does it in a way that's like, kind of crazy."

Mazzulla believes that sometimes it's the things you *don't* do that make the difference. "So many times people are focused on trying to win. I think it's just as important as keeping yourself from losing," he said. "And as hard as it is to win, it's very easy to lose. And just maintaining that balance—it's not always about winning. It's about making sure you have an understanding of what losing looks like and how easy it is to fall into particular habits that can lead to losing at some point. Winning is just as dangerous as losing and vice versa."

There's no doubt that Mazzulla is a serious, focused guy, but he understands the importance of his job to the rabid Celtics fanbase. "I mean, I wouldn't say I *enjoyed* the offseason," he said. "I enjoyed the parade. I thought the parade was a rather intense experience, which I loved, and it was a great opportunity to connect with the city. And No. 1 goal, one of my goals in being the head coach, is making sure we maintain the consistent mind-set and the consistent connection to the city of Boston, the chip on your shoulder, the toughness, the expectation to winning. So, I thought the parade was kind of a culmination of that connection."

Mazzulla saying he didn't enjoy the offseason isn't a surprise. When he was named Coach of the Month for March, Derrick White congratulated him. Mazzulla's response? "Nobody cares." That's our coach.

Holiday puts it simply. "Anybody who knows Joe knows he's crazy, and that's pretty much it," he said. "But I think it's maybe controlled madness. It's definitely his way of preparing us and, I feel, preparing himself."

He also isn't a guy that's going to walk away from giant expectations. "All those things go into making who you are as a person. If someone tells you, 'Good job,' that's just as dangerous as someone telling you [that you] suck," Mazzulla said. "You need both of them in order to get to where you want to get to, and there's no place else I'd rather be."

Mazzulla wants his team to be great, and he brings a really interesting point of view to things. He was asked about whether the loss to Miami Heat the previous year motivated his team during the championship season. "At the end of the day, whether we won or lost, if we're standing up here at this point, the goal is to win," he said. "If we would have lost last year, our goal would be to win a championship this year. I think just clearly stating we want to win a championship every single year—that's the goal. That's the standard. That's the expectation. So, what happened in the past really doesn't change when we step foot in the building on this day. It's to win a championship."

And make no mistake: these Celtics have been built in the image of their coach. "I feel like this type of team is Joe Mazzulla ball. It's defending and being gritty on offense," Horford said. "Everybody [is] a threat on the court at the same time. And everything that he wanted to do, he was able to accomplish. He always knew when to push the buttons. He's hard. He can be a little wacky sometimes, but that's what we appreciate about him. He truly cares about us, and he cares about what it means to be a Celtic."

Celtics management took a huge risk hiring an unknown back-row assistant to coach a championship-contending team. Outgoing team owner Wyc Grousbeck told *The Globe* that this was a gamble that has paid off in a huge way. "It's super satisfying to have everybody else see what we saw. I'm as happy for Joe as I am for anybody," he said. "I'm thrilled that his own unique brand of being the most intense, driven person I've ever met has translated into a championship. He's hilarious, and he's a winner, and he's our guy, and that's going to be a forever relationship."

Or maybe not *forever*. Mazzulla got a little morbid when asked about whether there's pressure with the job. "We're all going to be dead soon, and it really doesn't matter anymore. So, there's zero pressure. You're either going to win or you're not. And when you win, you try to forget about it a week later, and when you lose, you try to forget about it a week later. And so, it's not pressure; it's an opportunity. And we have an opportunity here over the next few years, however long we're together," he said. "We've said this in the past: we have an opportunity to carry the organization forward, to double down on the tradition and the history of what this organization has. And what else would you expect than someone expecting you to win all the time? I wouldn't want someone expecting me to lose all the time. That would be debilitating. So, we have an expectation to win."

CHAPTER TWENTY-SEVEN

DEFENDING THE TITLE

Thisis why Joe Mazzulla is our coach. Here's what he told the *Locked on Celtics* podcast: "The phrase 'defending a title' is a very passive-aggressive term. If you look at the animal kingdom, some of the strongest animals don't defend; they're the most aggressive and they attack the most. Whether you've won or haven't won, your mind-set can't change. You have to understand what goes into winning and losing, commit to the details on a daily basis, and remain aggressive. You're not defending something; you're attacking a new goal."

It doesn't really matter which sport you're talking about. There's nothing harder than defending a championship. Hall of Fame writer Bob Ryan pointed to three issues—injuries, complacency, and competition—that can derail a team from repeating.

Injuries

We won it in 1981 and had everything going for us to repeat. Robert Parish was in his fifth season, I was in my fourth, Larry Bird and Gerald Henderson were both in their second, and Kevin McHale was a rookie. Our only real veteran was Hall of Famer Nate "Tiny" Archibald. We were young, healthy, and full of hope. The year we won the title, we won 62 games during the regular season. The next year we won 63. In 1982 we added Danny Ainge; so, you had to figure we'd be better.

Both years we went down 3–1 in the Eastern Conference Finals to the Philadelphia 76ers. In 1981 we made a historic comeback to win and advance to the NBA Finals. The next year we came back to force Game Seven at the Boston Garden...and got drilled to end our season. What was the difference? In Game Three against Philly, Tiny went down with a dislocated shoulder just 83 seconds into the game. That was just too much for us to overcome.

Zoom ahead to 1984, and we beat the Los Angeles "Fakers" in seven games. We were still young: Chief was 30, Dennis Johnson was 29, Henderson and I were 28, Bird was 27, McHale was 26, and Ainge was 25. Again, we were the best team in the world. We were young, hungry, and healthy. Until we weren't.

I hurt my knee and wasn't right the entire season. I was only able to play 57 games, which was the fewest in my career to that point. Most importantly, I wasn't the same player and in the postseason—outside of one game against the Detroit Pistons—I was really not a factor, and we fell to the Lakers. (As a side note, I always find it weird when people say it was somehow my fault that we didn't win. I mean, we had four Hall of Famers: Bird, Chief, McHale, and D.J. We had another really good player in Ainge. And little old me was the reason we didn't repeat? The same guy who Red Auerbach played hardball with over contract negotiations the previous summer? Really? But I digress.) Once again, the injury bug did us in. The 1986 team was great, but Bill Walton got hurt, and the Boston Celtics didn't repeat. So, injuries are a bitch.

Looking at this current group, they're all young, but obviously the biggest injury question is with Kristaps Porzingis. If you tell me how many games he can play in the postseason, I'll tell you if the Celtics can repeat. But even including K.P., these guys are so talented, and other than Al Horford and Jrue Holiday, they're all just reaching their prime. If you do suffer an injury, you hope it's early. "You almost always want to start with injury and hope you stay healthy and don't lose a key player, for example, and maybe everything's different," Ryan said. "You have to depend on somebody who's aging and you want to age themselves out."

Complacency

Another challenge in repeating is focus. Probably the best example of this would be the 1985 Chicago Bears. They won the Super Bowl with one of the most dominant teams ever, but they also liked being celebrities. There was the "Super Bowl Shuffle" song, there were books, contract disputes. Even one of the greatest running backs of all time, Walter Payton, was pissed because Mike Ditka ran a trick play to let William "the Refrigerator" Perry score a touchdown in the Super Bowl while "Sweetness" didn't score. Think about that: the leading rusher in NFL history at the time didn't get into the end zone while a defensive tackle did. No wonder he was pissed.

What's great about this team is how Brad Stevens and the front office took care of things.

Jaylen Brown got his payday after they lost to the Miami Heat and became the highest-paid player in the sport. After the 2023–24 title, Jayson Tatum got his contract and became the highest-paid player in the sport. Before the playoffs even started, they locked up Holiday for another four years. In July Derrick White signed his four-year extension. And K.P.? They took care of him before he ever played a game in Boston. As you can imagine, money is a major issue when you're dealing with a team, and the Celtics are all settled in that category. And after Brown and Tatum's issues with the Olympics, complacency shouldn't be a problem.

Competition

The NBA, like most sports leagues, is all about copycats. If you didn't win, you want to try and find a way to get better. That could include signing a big free agent like Paul George in Philadelphia or the New York Knicks trading for Mikal Bridges and Karl-Anthony Towns.

One thing that's cool about this Celtics team is they worry about themselves—no one else. When you're the most talented team, if you do your job, you should win. As you'd expect, the 2024 champions had a plan coming into the new season. "Joe, he had a great quote the other day," Tatum said. "He said, 'We're not defending anything. We're chasing another championship.' We enjoyed it all summer. We enjoyed it during training camp. I can't wait for opening night to get our rings and see the banner being raised. But, honestly, after opening night we have to put it behind us. It's a new season. Last year was last year. We accomplished something special.

We've got to figure out a way to get better. We wanted to approach the game with the same mind-set, and we did an amazing job of that last year. Not to toot our own horn, but we were pretty good [last season]. We believed it."

People around the NBA believe in what's going in Boston. Former coach/current broadcaster Stan Van Gundy told *The Boston Globe* that he's buying what the team is selling—both on offense and more importantly on defense. "There were times when people criticized them: too one-dimensional, too many threes. But what sort of misses in that analysis is that team leans on their defense to win games. That is probably the best NBA roster I've seen. All five guys can defend," he said. "Their top guys and their starters, forget it. Every one of them is a plus defender, and there's no one in their top eight that you don't have to guard. I've never seen a team like that."

* * *

Tooting your own horn is something to keep an eye on, too. So many teams win and think they're unbeatable. Brad Stevens said it's critical to remember how hard it was to win the title because it's only going to be more difficult. "It's a little bit ironic when considered that everywhere else you go you're being told how great you are. And I think you just have to balance it with what's real," Stevens said. "And what's real is the margin for error of winning is small, and you have to give everything you have every day to be the best you can every time you take that court...But the question is how can we stay consistent and are we about the things that we embraced last year to get there? Do we sacrifice for one another? Are we willing to take everybody's best shot? Do we look at it as a fun challenge? For me this is as good of a challenge as you get if you're a competitor. So, we should be excited about it."

One thing that is a great sign is that everyone in the organization is working off of the same playbook. They remember the success obviously but haven't forgotten the heartache.

"Everybody's excited, especially, I mean, we've got the same team back and guys that we've won a lot of games together…We've experienced obviously the highest of joy, but we've also experienced those defeats that kind of managed the team and the players that we are today," Derrick White said. "When you go through things like that together, and then obviously we've got great people that you want to play for and you want to play as teammates, and so I think it's just a lot of excitement just to get back to it, and I'm looking forward to it."

When you look at great teams, a common thread is that your best players are on the same page as the coach, and Joe Mazzulla is as driven as anyone in the NBA. Here's his philosophy about getting back to the basics: "At the end of the day, if we don't go back to those fundamentals and assume that just because we have everybody back, we're going to do the littlest of things. That's when you get in trouble," he said. "So we start from square one, start all over again. And I think over time that continuity will pick up, but you got to start from scratch."

Compare that to Tatum's take. "The important thing is being proud of what we did last season, and last year was amazing," he said. "We were an incredible team, and we made history. And this year not necessarily feeling like we have to defend the title, but we're trying to go win it. We had a target on our back the last couple of years. You know nothing has changed in that aspect. If anything, we know how great it felt to win and what it took and we're trying to go win again."

When you get your best players to buy in and on the same page as their coach, you're going to be successful. "How open-minded can we be to get back up to speed on our reads, communication, our connectivity on both ends of the floor?" Mazzulla asked. "They've done that. That sets you up to be able to handle what the season has in store for you."

Tatum's sidekick has an interesting point of view about the razor-thin difference between winning it all and losing. "The year before when we lost, it was the lowest of lows for me. I felt like it was my responsibility when we lost in Game Seven and kind of fell short," Jaylen Brown said. "And now it feels like we won, and it was the same kind of deal but just opposite ends of the spectrum. But it kind of feels the same if you look at them in hindsight because you can go one way or another in both of those directions. When you're at the bottom, you can go one way or when you're at the top you can keep going up or you can go down. So, it feels weirdly, oddly the same."

Coach Mazzulla also preached about the danger of believing you've figured everything out. "Having an expectation that it's going to go a certain way, also thinking because we've done it one way, we just have to do it that way again, right? And I think that's a challenge heading into any season," he said.

"There's obviously principles, non-negotiables, things that we have to recreate, that we have to do every single year. And then there's things that we got to adjust and find ways to be better. So I think the challenge comes into just coming into this season with a closed mind-set. We have to have an open mind. We've got to have an understanding of our environment's changed. And we have to change."

I think this group—management and players—is going about this the right way. Now that they've finally burst that psychological bubble, they're in great shape to win multiple championships. Everyone is coming after them, but at the end of the day, I still think they're head and shoulders above the rest of the league.

CHAPTER TWENTY-EIGHT

OLYMPIC GAMES

After you win a championship, the following summer is always short. Guys celebrate, do endorsements, take vacations, those kinds of things. It's one of the reasons it's so hard to repeat.

In the summer of 2024, a few of the Boston Celtics were busy representing their country at the Olympics. Obviously, Kristaps Porzingis wasn't going to be able to play for his native Latvia, as he was recovering from ankle surgery. Jayson Tatum and Jrue Holiday were selected for Team USA; that much we knew. But when Kawhi Leonard was sent home to rehabilitate his knee, there was an open spot.

Hmmm, who could fill that role of a great two-way player with a winning pedigree and good work ethic? Everyone thought it would be Jaylen Brown. I mean the guy just won the title and was named MVP of the Eastern Conference Finals and NBA Finals. He'd played on the Team USA World Cup team in 2019. It was a no-brainer. Until it wasn't.

Hall of Famer Grant Hill is the managing director for the men's basketball team. Between him, coach Steve Kerr, and whoever else they spoke with, they decided to skip Brown and invited Derrick White to the team instead. Obviously, this is no knock on D-White. He fits with any group, but Brown clearly took it as a slap in the face. First, he tweeted out a post saying, "This what we doing?"

Of course, I was surprised that they picked D-White over J.B., but you have to understand what the Olympics are: a Nike event. It makes the best basketball shoe in the world and has the most popular brand in the world. Nike is sponsoring the Olympics; so, you know they're going to make sure they pick players who represent them. Back in 2022 Nike cut ties with Kyrie Irving over some anti-Semitic remarks. Brown defended Irving, and Nike got pissed. So, Brown was a sneaker free agent and had rebuffed Nike's efforts.

Another theory was that since that World Cup team only finished sixth, Hill wanted a clean slate. Al Horford had his teammate's back, telling ESPN, "You saw an evolution in Jaylen's game [last season]," he said. "It wasn't just about scoring. He was getting people involved. He's making the right reads. He is making the cuts when he needs to make it to the basket. And then on the defensive end, he just took it to another level. His energy, his commitment to the defense—it was inspiring for all of us."

The public furor was great enough that Hill had to address it. "You get 12 spots, and you have to build a team. And one of the hardest things is leaving people off the roster that I'm a fan of," Hill said. "But the responsibility that I have is to put together a team that will give us the best opportunity for success, and so whatever theories that might be out there, they're just that."

By the way, what type of shirt do you think Hill was wearing when he said this? A Nike one! Brown——never one to mince words—had his last say. "Grant Hill calling me a conspiracy theorist is disappointing I've been a VP [in the players' union] since I was 21 years old. I have a great understanding."

Hill tried to clean things up but probably made it worse, saying, "For a good portion of my career, I wore Fila. That was supposed to be a joke. We're proud of our partners obviously…this is about putting together a team."

To which J.B. responded on X: "I'm not afraid of you and your resources."

When asked if he thought the Nike issue was at the root of his snub, Brown told The Athletic: "I do for sure. There will be more stuff to come with that. As of now, I'm not gonna comment on it."

Hill then appeared on the All the Smoke's *Open Run,* a podcast with Rachel Nichols, and seemed to be trying to make nice. "I'm confident he and I will sit down at some point and talk about it and get to some level of understanding," Hill said. "Look, he'll be a candidate if he wants in '28."

He was then asked if he'd be okay with Brown on the 2028 team in Los Angeles. "Oh, yeah," Hill said, "one thing I've learned. You can't take anything personal in this role. And so, I haven't personalized anything. My goal, my objective is to win. As soon as hopefully that happens, we pivot and start looking ahead to the future."

I'm sure there's more to come on this one. Most importantly to Brown, he wanted to make sure his teammate knew this wasn't anything at all against him, telling reporters during the NBA Summer League, "I called Derrick right away, just to make sure there's no confusion, my love for you, and all of that," he said. "He knew that, and he did. You don't always got to make everything public. Me and D-White are good."

The sentiment was shared by his teammate. "No, there's no elephants in there," White said. "That was never an issue. That was never really needed to be talked about."

Of course, the very first question Brown was asked on Media Day was about not getting that Olympic invite. He handled it in stride. "Damn, question No. 1?" Brown asked, laughing. "Can't warm up a little? Shit." A lot of guys wouldn't have taken it so well, but after the year Brown just had, he can afford to chuckle.

With that snub settled, we all figured it would be a quiet Olympics for our guys. We couldn't be more wrong. Back in the 2020–21 games, Tatum played 20 minutes per game, averaging 15 points, as the U.S. won the gold medal. A few years later, he's obviously a much better player, an NBA champion, and has been first-team All-NBA for the past three seasons. During that time he's also finished in the top six for MVP. You'd *think* he'd be featured in the 2024 games in Paris. No sir. Tatum was almost an afterthought, even sitting out two games, including Team USA's semifinal win against Serbia. I know everyone wanted to kill Kerr for not giving minutes to J.T., but he had a job: to win a gold medal. He didn't do the friend zone thing. He just coached, and I admire that.

You can't play everyone, which is something Brad Stevens learned in 2018. Think about the guys on that roster: the Jays, Kyrie Irving, Gordon Hayward, Terry Rozier, Marcus Smart. To be honest, this was one of the most stacked teams I've seen in the league. I think that wore Stevens out. The current

Celtics squad is great about that. Take a guy like Payton Pritchard. He might play; he might not. But if he plays two minutes, we know he's going to play hard.

This was the hand Coach Kerr was dealt—12 truly great players, 40-minute games. There was no way to keep everyone happy. I know I'm in the minority when it comes to defending Coach Kerr. More people thought like *The Boston Globe*'s Bob Ryan, a self-described fan of Kerr. "It was a somewhat specious argument that the math doesn't work, that you can't do it," he said. "You *can* do it. You can sit them all down before it starts. 'I've got 12 All-Stars, you're all great players, you're all going to get your moments, you're all going to get to play. Some nights you're not going to play as much as you want, and some nights the sky will be your star.'"

Ryan says he heard reports that Tatum hadn't been playing well in practices, that his shot had deserted him. Then there was the Kevin Durant factor. "When Durant had that spectacular first game [23 points in 17 minutes against Serbia], you've got to figure that they were slotted in the same kind of mind-set on the court by Kerr," Ryan continues. "I think Durant made it an easier decision for him."

Obviously, that team is stacked, and, I mean, Tatum could have thrown a fit, but he just did his thing. That's great. This is the thing I love about that kid here. He's a great kid. He's a great person. I was talking with Tatum during training camp and I told him how proud I am of him. I then asked why so many people were hating on him. Think about the guy they're attacking. He just won his second Olympic gold, won his first NBA title, got a huge contract, and had a new baby. Tatum just looked at me and said, "Man, I don't know. I am so happy, and I am so blessed." That was so great to hear him say that and for him to see the forest for the trees.

Did he have confidence in Paris? Not really. He didn't have his usual swagger. J.T. took a back seat to guys like Durant and LeBron James, which I have no problem with. And at the end of the day, nothing else should have mattered. Tatum earned a gold medal, not a participation trophy. "I know I didn't make a jump shot when I was with Team USA. I don't know, law of averages," Tatum said. "It's a weird rhythm thing being with Team USA; you never exactly know when you're gonna get the ball, but that's part of it. You sign up for that because I've done it before [at the Tokyo Games]. I'm always a glass-half-full type of guy. I always believe everything happens for a reason, and whatever that is, I don't know yet. But I'm certain I'll find out."

Although he did win his second gold medal, Tatum was an afterthought, scoring five points and adding five rebounds per game. To his credit, Tatum put on a good face during the games, but at least publicly, he's not letting Kerr's decision shape his narrative. "Did I need any extra motivation coming into the season? No, I don't. I'm not gonna give anybody in particular credit that they're motivating me to come into the season," he said. "It was a unique circumstance. Something I [haven't] experienced before in my playing career, but I'm a believer that everything happens for a reason. I was coming off a championship, the highest of the highs, a *2K* cover, and a new contract, and then that happened and whatever the reason is I haven't figured out yet."

And being the leader he is, Joe Mazzulla reached out to his star. Tatum joked that his coach was actually happy that he didn't win Finals MVP or play in two games of the Olympics, figuring it would give him motivation. "I mean, that's just the way that I love him and the relationship that we have. I appreciate that he accepts my perspective and the way that we go about talking about it," Mazzulla explained. "Sometimes when you get success, you don't have that next hunger right in front of you. Sometimes you've got to wait for it. Sometimes it's a loss. Sometimes it's a losing streak. And he was able to get that right in front of him. So I just thought it was a gift. It doesn't mean that he shouldn't be pissed off about it. I didn't want to take away from how that may affect him in real time. So I wasn't there. But as his coach and as somebody that really cares about him, I thought it was great. It gives him something to work for."

Tatum took the high road. He praised the Olympic experience. "We won the gold medal. I won my second one," he said. "I was around some of the best players that ever played a game on a daily basis and built some friendships and was able to bring my family out there and enjoy the Olympics as a whole. So that was a plus for me for sure."

After Brown's snub and Tatum's lack of playing time, the old veteran on the team had both of their backs. "I personally was not happy about it," Horford told ESPN. "Those guys, they're very special to me. And even though it was nothing against me, it motivated me and all of us for this season."

That's why this team is so successful; they really do play for each other.

CHAPTER TWENTY-NINE

BANNER 18— ONE MORE THAN L.A.

B eing a champion is great. Having the most titles in NBA history—ahead of the Los Angeles Lakers— is even better. A lot better. Those brothers thought they were all that when they won the inaugural in-season tournament; they even hung a banner for it! Let me say that I *cannot* wait to wear my championship ring to one place—Los Angeles. I want to make sure Mychal Thompson gets to see it.

When guys like Thompson, Michael Cooper, James Worthy, and I get together, we are like old soldiers, who swear like sailors. A lot of "MFs" and "bitches" going around. I tell them how they couldn't guard me. Of course, these days we can't guard anyone. I'm pretty sure none of us can even dunk with the possible exception of my good friend Robert Parish. I know Kareem Abdul-Jabbar ain't doing it, Magic Johnson ain't doing it, Worthy ain't doing it, and I sure as hell ain't doing it.

I'd love to see us rip off a few more titles, so we have that cushion. Maybe the Boston Celtics winning is good for the Lakers; so, now they don't have to focus on the in-season "championship" and can try to get as many titles as us. That's all they can do because they can't pass us in one year. Regarding that in-season tourney, I was talking to Hall of Famer Mo Cheeks, now an assistant with the New York Knicks. I asked how he'd like playing one game, where the winners all get $500,000. He smiled, and I said, "I know there would be some dead people on the floor."

* * *

It's always tough to compare teams and/or players from different eras. Each era has its own rules and trends. Bob Ryan has covered six championships in his media career. For the legendary sportswriter, there's no question which Boston Celtics team is the best of all time—the 1986 title winners. Larry Bird, Kevin McHale, Robert Parish, and Dennis Johnson all ended up in the Basketball Hall of Fame. But the special sauce for this group in Ryan's opinion was the addition of Bill Walton (who was traded for me)! "There's never been a sixth man coming off the bench to change the game the way Bill Walton did, and no team ever had the luxury of having two Hall of Fame centers on the team at the same time," Ryan said. "And one of them [Parish] at the peak of his career, and the other one, you know…"

Yes, I know. The Celtics made a deal with the devil (in this case, the Los Angeles Clippers) to get one healthy year out of Walton, which they did. After winning the title that season—and playing in a career-high 80 games—Walton got hurt the next training camp, played in 10 more games, and that was it. The backstory of how Walton got to Boston is interesting.

He wanted to play for the Celtics so badly that he called Red Auerbach directly, pleading his case. I was coming off my serious knee injury in 1985 and was pissed because so many people thought I didn't want to play, which was total bullshit. In my immaturity I decided I wanted out, which made a trade with the Clippers that much easier.

I went out to L.A. and failed my physical. I then spent a month out there getting my knee in shape so I could pass. Walton, on the other hand, also failed his physical. By this point, though, the Celtics didn't really care. They just wanted to get him, and miraculously Walton ended up passing. My injury had given Auerbach the opportunity to consider dealing me. He saw the future—what McHale was becoming as a player—and couldn't put him back on the bench. I would have been fine coming off the bench, but the word was the team didn't want to do that because I'd create a stink and didn't want to play.

That misconception really pissed me off. Before the trade was official, Auerbach talked to Parish to make sure he was cool with another big man coming in. Chief said Auerbach told him he wanted to trade me for those reasons, but Parish had my back and told him that was total bullshit, how I was as competitive as anyone on this team. It wasn't like I was faking it—you can't fake out your body. I couldn't run; that was a fact.

That edition of the Celtics went an incredible 40–1 at Boston Garden, winning the last 13 games at home by an average of 17 points. To Ryan there's no question that was the best team of all time. "Oh, they are the No. 1. I mean, there ain't this issue who's going to be No. 1, and no one should ever have any doubts about that," he stated clearly, adding that he doesn't know how any other team can possibly match up. "I don't know what's going to do it because nobody's going to come back with Robert, Kevin, and Larry, and Bill Walton."

Wait a minute. I love when people say this is the greatest team of all time. I'm not hating, but I say, "They won how many championships?" One. To be considered an all-time great team, don't you have to win multiple titles? Apparently not. Was their season magical? Absolutely. They lost one home game. Who did that team beat to win the title? The Houston Rockets. Go back to Shaquille O'Neal's comment about how easy the path was for the 2024 Celtics. Does that apply to 1986? They were all geared up to play the Los Angeles Lakers for the third year in a row, but Ralph Sampson hit a lucky shot, and L.A. was gone.

If you want to say the '86 team was the best in one season, that's different. Look at the 1972 Miami Dolphins. They are still the only team to finish the season (and playoffs) without losing a single game. Yet when people talk about the best teams in the NFL history, most aren't picking Miami. But for that one single season, it was magical. Whenever I'm asked about which was the all-time best team, I mean, how do you top the Celtics teams from 1959 to 1966? They won *eight* straight championships! You think anyone is ever coming close to that?

* * *

I was asked how the 2024 Boston Celtics compared with our first championship group in 1981. It's *so* hard to compare eras. I mean the easiest difference to point out is that these

Finals were on live TV. When we won in 1981, the games were on tape delay! Then there are the expectations. In 1981 we knew that the real NBA Finals were when we played the Philadelphia 76ers in the Eastern Conference Finals. Whoever won that series was definitely going to take home the title—especially with a Houston Rockets team that had a losing record advancing from the West.

In 2024 everyone was waiting for the other shoe to drop. Even in Game Five, the Celtics were up by 25 points against the Dallas Mavericks, and in the back of people's minds, they were thinking, *They're going to let them back in.* I mean, they were up 3–1 in the series! That's why I say this team was like Rodney Dangerfield—they never got any respect. It was always because this guy was hurt or that one.

The bottom line is that the Celtics were the best team in the league all season long, and they won the championship. End of discussion. Then in 1984 we had obviously already won a title and then faced the Los Angeles "Fakers" in the Finals. Talk about a heavyweight matchup! The TV ratings were 19.3, an NBA record. Nothing against the Mavericks, but they ain't the Lakers.

But one of the cool things about this group is that their place in history is still incomplete.

Think about the things we don't know. Does Jayson Tatum go down this path for the rest of his career? Does Jaylen Brown use his Finals MVP as a springboard to enter the next level of stardom? Are those guys destined to be Hall of Famers? Will they go down as the greatest book-end set of forwards—better than Larry Bird and Kevin

McHale? Hell, better than Bird and Cedric Maxwell? And what about Kristaps Porzingis? Think about how the perception of him changed in just one season. It reminds me of Robert Parish. When he was on the Golden State Warriors, the word was that he was lazy and didn't want to play. He came to Boston, won a championship, and is now in the Hall of Fame.

The talent on the current Celtics is ridiculous, but as we all know, talent isn't the only thing that matters. When you look at the Lakers of the 1980s, they were oozing with talent: Kareem Abdul-Jabbar, Magic Johnson, James Worthy, etc. We weren't as talented, but we *played* basketball and were crazy tough. That's how we beat them in 1984.

I don't think you can even look at this team and think about how they rank talent-wise with some of the great teams that have been in Celtics history because you just don't have enough information on them. That said, *The Boston Globe*'s Bob Ryan made a statement that might raise eyebrows regarding the 2024 Celtics. "In context of their time, these Celtics have the deepest collection of legitimate NBA players on their roster of any team in NBA history," he said. "They have the best one through five, the best one through eight, the best one through 10. The deepest team of all time."

Ryan stressed "the context of their time" because he doesn't believe the 2024 champions would beat the 1986 squad, but his point is well taken. Aside from the starters, to be able to bring guys like Payton Pritchard, Luke Kornet, and Sam Hauser off the bench makes a huge difference.

"It's jumped in out at me. I just never have been struck by it the way I was with this group," Ryan said. "And it's incredible roster assembly just by Danny and Brad."

I'd have to agree with Ryan in the sense that when you start looking at these guys, you've got two monster forwards who are just killing everyone. Add Kristaps Porzingis, who is a nightmare matchup for anyone. Lastly, it's the best defensive backcourt in NBA history. There's no weakness on this team. That's what makes them that much more dangerous than anyone.

CHAPTER THIRTY

THE RING CEREMONY

Though the crowning event of any championship is the raising of the banner and the presentation of the rings. I always think it's a bit anticlimactic, though, as you win on the floor and celebrate. Then months later you do the banner and rings. It's like you want to move forward and start the new season, but you have to look back and appreciate what you've done.

As usual, the organization did things the right way. It was great that 96-year-old Bob Cousy was on hand to bridge the generations. Cousy had promised that he'd be there no matter what, and he always keeps his promises. Yours truly represented the 1980s, and Kevin Garnett, Paul Pierce, and Ray Allen showed out for the 2008 team.

The rings were, of course, huge, with a detachable top that covers an actual piece of the Boston Garden's parquet. Such a weird dynamic—they give out the rings, which the players loved—then they have to give them back so they can play! I was speaking with Jaylen Brown and told him, "I haven't had a chance to tell you congratulations on the Finals MVP."

J.B. responded, "It takes one to know one!" *That* was very cool.

"I mean, that ring is just an object, right?" Brown said. "But it's the everything—the emotions, the heartbreak, the embarrassment, the work, the drive, the dedication. That's what that ring represents."

I also had a chance to chat with Xavier Tillman, and he was just absolutely giddy. I said, "Man, you're grinning like a chicken."

He said, "Do you *see* the size of this ring? Do you see that?"

It's always really cool to see guys' reactions to getting their jewelry. As everyone was called up to get the rings, Joe Mazzulla stole the show by getting on all fours and kissing the parquet. "I just thought that was a moment, a way for me to just express myself," he said. "That parquet is where there's blood, sweat, and tears of the greats. I don't get to go out there and dive on the floor for loose balls like I'd love to or do any of that; so, that was a way to just express the passion and the gratitude that I have for our team, for the people that have come before, and for what it means to be a Celtic."

The whole night was incredible, and the fact that the team tied an NBA record with 29 three-pointers in blowing out the New York Knicks was even better.

ACKNOWLEDGMENTS

Shemeka Maxwell, Doctor Morgan Maxwell, Madison Maxwell, and Devin Maxwell, your support and love over the years has been my greatest joy. Now to the woman who saw the vision, Bessie Maxwell. My wonderful mother saw the basketball player in me when nobody else recognized it. Your passion for competing has helped me countless ways—whether it was basketball, bid whist, *Monopoly*, *Sorry!*, or any game I've ever played.

—*C.M.*

This is my fourth book with Triumph (fifth overall), and I couldn't even think about accomplishing this without the love and support of my family. My wife, Katie, always gives me the space and time to undertake projects that I'm passionate about. My (no longer) children, Zach and Cookie Isenberg, make me so proud as they pursue their dreams in Chicago. The support they constantly give isn't always talked about but is always appreciated! My two dog children, Toby and Matilda, get excited when I do interviews—sometimes louder than others, LOL—but always enthusiastic. Whenever I need to focus on writing, Toby is constantly by my side. He's my guy.

The tight turnaround from winning the title to getting a manuscript done in time made this the toughest project I've undertaken. The cast of folks we spoke to were incredibly important to the process. Relationships with Bob Ryan and Dan Shaughnessy from previous projects were critical in getting this book off the ground. Boston Celtics president Brad Stevens carved out time to chat—even in the heat of trying to prepare for defense of their title. Joe Mazzulla gave us time early in the 2024 campaign. Assistant general manager Austin Ainge was more than generous with his time as well.

Most importantly, thank you to my coauthor, Cedric Maxwell. Completing two books with a guy I grew up idolizing has been such a thrill. Max is always generous with his time and *never* has a filter. He's a champion on and *off* the court, and I am proud to call him a friend.

—*M.I.*

© Katie Isenberg